MW01282713

LVE GAME

STORIES THAT INSPIRE FROM MY TWELVE YEARS AROUND THE WORLD INSIDE PRO TENNIS

FRITZ GLAUS
WITH MIKE YORKEY

▲ Levita Media

Love Game

Photography: Robin Glaus

Back cover photo: Fritz and Robin Glaus enjoying a match
at Court Central at Roland Garros in Paris, France

Cover Design by Jason Able
Page Layout by Pauline Scoggins
Levita Media
www.levitamedia.com

Printed in the United States of America

For more information: www.lovegamebook.com

A NOTE FROM FRITZ GLAUS

I would like to dedicate the book to everyone who made my ministry on the professional tennis tour possible. As you look at the pictures and read the stories, it's obvious that my time on the tour could never have taken place without the love, support, and prayers of people all over the world.

Financial supporters, housing families, local tennis pros, churches, and sports ministries around the world each played a role in weaving a beautiful tapestry that spanned twelve years. The ripple effect of those years continues on today, through the individuals whose lives were impacted and the lives they now touch.

My wife, Robin, and I are forever grateful.

ACKNOWLEDGMENTS

Thanks to Wayne Cooper and the
Elevation Church Writers in the Spirit eGroup
for inspiring and supporting this project.
www.WritersInTheSpirit.com

CONTENTS

Speaking

If you would like to book Fritz and Robin Glaus for a speaking engagement, please direct your inquiries to:
info@fritzglaus.com

www.FritzGlaus.com

Discover More Online

www.LoveGameBook.com

Fresh out of college, I was ready to see the world.

1
FIRST SERVE

Key Biscayne, 1991. I took my courtside seat at the Crandon Park Tennis Center, the newly minted 13,300-seat stadium court that was home of the Lipton International Players Championship.

It was a typical day for South Florida in mid-March; the early afternoon sun baked the thousands of tennis fans with a warm-but-not-too-hot 81 degrees. Already, though, the high humidity precipitated rings of sweat to soak through my white Sergio Tachini polo shirt trimmed with red and green piping.

One of my players was taking his five-minute warm-up on the stadium court prior to the start of his early-round match. I don't say *my player* because I was coaching him, at least in how he stroked the ball or how he should play his opponent. Instead, I felt an emotional bond because I was helping him search for something more meaningful in life than hitting a fuzzy optic yellow tennis ball.

You see, I was a chaplain on the men's ATP professional tennis tour, traveling ten months a year conducting twice-weekly Bible studies, meeting one-on-one with players, forming friendships in the locker rooms with players—and watching a ton of tennis matches, including this second round matchup.

One thing I had noticed over the years was how some players, even if they professed to be Christians, were as superstitious as Art "Tappy" Larsen, a top U.S. player from the amateur days of the 1950s. Larsen was nicknamed "Tappy" because he clung to the belief that good things would happen to him if he tapped on objects. He tapped everything in sight: the white lines with his racket, the umpire's stand, or top of the net. When he changed his clothes before a match, he tapped his leg as he put on a pair of tennis shorts; as he slipped on his sneakers, he tapped the floor; and as he hung his pants in his locker, he tapped the wooden frame for good luck.

None of the players I interacted with were as superstitious as Tappy Larsen, but more than a few made sure they tapped the ground with their racket whenever they sat down during the changeover. Others wore the same socks to each match or ate at the same restaurant when they were on a winning streak. One player insisted that I sit in a certain spot for each of his matches, knowing that if I was there pulling for him, he'd play better and get through to the next round.

I didn't want to be anyone's lucky charm, however, so I made sure I moved around during his matches. Another reason I didn't like to plant myself in a particular spot was that I wanted the freedom to move around the tournament grounds. In the early rounds of most tournaments, I usually watched up to a half-dozen players—the ones who were either regularly attending our Bible studies or were talking to me about what it meant to be a Christian—play for their livelihood. I felt like viewing their matches was my job so I would know what they were going through. You see, winning and losing is everything in professional tennis. Win, and the world loves you and showers you with tons of money and fame. Lose early or lose often, and you're quickly forgotten.

It didn't take me long to figure out that professional tennis was a tough gig. Tennis is a meritocracy that brutally cuts the field in half with each round, so if I wanted to see all my players, I had to do a lot of moving around in the first and second rounds.

Even though I worked with players near the top of the rankings, I wanted to show just as much interest with the journeymen trying to scratch out a few wins so they could keep their ranking up and still get into the Grand Slam tournaments—where the real money was waiting to be made.

Sitting in the coach's box at the Lipton tournament that March afternoon, though, watching the players loosen up, I thought how far I'd come—and how much of the world I had seen—during the last twelve years as a tennis chaplain. If you had told me in 1976 after I graduated from college that I would be traveling the world on the professional tennis tour, leading Bible studies, organizing housing for players with Christian families, or developing friendships with some of the most famous tennis players in the world, I would have thought you were a bit daft, as they would say in the British newspapers.

But I did get a chance to fulfill my dream, and from early 1980 until the fall of 1992, I ministered to hundreds of players on the men's professional tennis tour. It was quite a ride, but it all happened because God had a hand on my life, as you shall soon see.

In the late 1980s, my wife, Robin, and I took a pilgrimage to my
birthplace in Andermatt, Switzerland. Believe it or not, I was born in
the stone house pictured behind us with a midwife in attendance.
Robin was born three years later in modern Broward General Hospital
in Fort Lauderdale, Florida.

Roots in Switzerland

You may be wondering how I got the name Fritz Glaus
because it is an unusual name for an American.

Actually, I am a naturalized American and was born
August 29, 1954, in the small mountain garrison of
Andermatt, high in the Swiss Alps. I'm named after my
father, Fritz Glaus, who was a Swiss dairyman serving in the
Swiss Army when I was born. He met my mother, Barbara,
at a local restaurant where she worked as a waitress. Mom
was Austrian, having fled the country just before the end of
World War II in search of a better life. They married in 1948,
and their first child, a daughter, arrived three years later.
They named her Barbara after my mom.

It soon became apparent that something was not right about young Barbara. Medical care was rudimentary in those days; Switzerland in the 1950s was still a landlocked country of diary farmers and goat shepherds eking out a living on the steep terrain and Alpine meadows. The Swiss tourism and high-tech industries were still a good twenty years away.

Doctors had bad news for my parents: it seemed that Barbara was mentally retarded and would never progress beyond the mental capacity of a six-year-old. This news hit my father like a ton of bricks. As for Mom, it's hard to say because my mother did not have all her cups in the cupboard either, as the Swiss are fond of saying. Mom wasn't 100 percent mentally there, even though she obviously functioned at a lot higher level than her daughter.

Doctors strongly urged my parents not to have any more children because they feared that any more offspring would be born just as mentally challenged. How much they listened, I do not know since both are dead now and they didn't like to talk about such matters when they were alive. The fact is that Mom became pregnant with me three years later. In another era, I would have probably become an abortion statistic, but in those days, my parents played the cards that had been dealt to them.

I think it was a miracle of God that I was born and that I came out normal. When I was thirty-five years old, I returned to Andermatt to visit my birthplace. In the late 1980s, Andermatt was a charming resort village of 1,500 residents in Central Switzerland. I found City Hall and asked the fellow behind the desk if he had any records of me being born in 1954. Within a few minutes, the clerk found the correct book for 1954 and found my date. It turns out that August 29, 1954, was a busy day for the local midwife; I was one of three

During my visit to Andermatt, Switzerland, I stopped by the town hall and found my birthdate listed in the official records.

children born that day in Andermatt. The clerk handed me a copy of my birth certificate, which I cherish to this day.

I only lived in Switzerland for two years. My parents decided to immigrate to America because of the opportunities for a better life and because they were told that there was special education available for young Barbara. We settled in Brewster, Ohio, a farmland area about thirty minutes southwest of Canton. A large Swiss contingent had immigrated to small rural towns in Ohio like Burton City and Dalton, where they either farmed or started dairy operations. Dad, a dairyman by profession, didn't want to milk cows anymore. He found a job at Nickles Bakery in nearby Navarre, founded by a Swiss immigrant named Alfred Nickles in 1909.

Nickles was a large industrial bakery that produced the

usual items for nearby markets and restaurants: enriched white bread, dinner rolls, whole grain breads, hot dog and hamburger buns, sweet rolls, cakes, and donuts. Many Swiss worked at Nickles, where they put in long ten-hour days from 4 a.m. to 2 p.m. Dad had a hard job and frequently complained of about being seared by the intense heat when he placed rows of bread into the hot ovens. If he breathed in the intense air, the heat would sear his nostrils.

When Dad came home from a long shift of baking breads and buns, he wasn't in the mood to talk. He'd flop into his big chair and read the paper. He spoke gruffly to me in Swiss-German, but I always responded in English—the language outside my front door. That bothered him, but what could he do? I was growing up in America and once I stepped outside, all my friends spoke English. Plus everything in school was in English.

Mom's English was worse than Dad's. She employed German and English words intermittently, and because of her limited mental capacity, she never became very fluent. Somehow she managed when she shopped, but she didn't have many friends on the block because she couldn't carry on a meaningful conversation with them. She stood around five feet, four inches and weighed about ninety pounds. Mom smoked most of her life, which led to her losing one lung. She certainly had trouble breathing, and I can certainly remember her hacking in spasmodic coughing.

Since I had turned out normal, my parents decided to have another child, but this time, their luck ran out. Something didn't add up with my younger brother, Peter, as well. He was mentally challenged—the victim of something called *neurofibromatosis*. It's hard to describe what it was like having two mentally challenged kids under one roof because that's all I knew growing up. But I haven't forgotten how I was teased in the schoolyard for having siblings in special education classes at our local school. School kids called them horrible names, like "retard" and "spaz material," and they constantly laughed in my face, like their existence was my fault.

I know that having two kids who weren't 100 percent wore Dad down. If something set him off, he'd take his frustrations out on me and whip me with his black belt. He and Mom also yelled a lot at each other, so there was constant

My family, circa 1960: (from the left) Dad, my sister Barbara, Mom, and my younger brother Peter and me.

tension inside our home. One can only imagine the irritations they endured with two mentally handicapped children underfoot and almost no support from social service agencies, which didn't exist in the late 1950s or early 1960s.

As for home life, Mom wasn't much of a cook. Dinner was the same meal every day — soft, overcooked noodles mixed with a bit of meat and white sauce. I have no idea what kind of meat Mom used. If we ever went out to eat in a restaurant, which was rare, we always ordered ham. My parents were creatures of habit.

As I got older, I didn't like getting swatted for doing nothing, so I made myself scarce during the daylight hours. Throughout my elementary school days, I usually hung out at Jeff Niedenthal's place. Jeff had two brothers, and they didn't mind setting an extra place at the table, so I ate dinner there as much as I could. During the long summer days, I spent as much time as possible at Jeff's house.

The desire to keep my parents at arm's length continued right into high school, so Dad got back at me. One Saturday night, I stayed out late with my friends at a dance club. I didn't get home until 2 a.m.

Ninety minutes later, at 3:30 a.m., Dad was banging on my bedroom door. "Get up! You're working this morning!" he barked in Swiss-German.

Dad had gotten me a job as a "sanitation engineer" at Nickles. He hadn't asked if I wanted the janitorial job, but he told me that I was taking it. My job was to clean the factory toilets. There were a lot of them because the Nickles bakery was five blocks long and employed hundreds of employees since Nickles bread products were sold throughout much of Ohio.

I counted the number of toilets one time: there were more

than 200. Dad usually signed me up to work on weekends, but sometimes I was so fatigued from staying out late with friends and getting roused out of bed before 4 a.m. that I'd fall asleep in one of the restrooms. My supervisor — who seemed to get a kick out of making my life miserable — would find me taking a snooze and tell me that I wasn't leaving until every single toilet at Nickles was spic and span — Swiss clean.

I didn't mind earning some money, however, because I wanted to buy my own car and enjoy the freedom that wheels could bring a high school teenager. I bought a '65 Ford Mustang fastback and thought that having my own car was great until the time when I backed out of the garage while the garage door was still down. That accident happened at four in the morning while I was on my way to work — after two hours of sleep. Dad cut me some slack and made me pay for only half of the damages, but I learned an important lesson.

Taking Up Tennis

There was another incident during my high school years where Dad showed a tender side. One time, Dad was supposed to get me tickets for the Cleveland Indians game that night, but he forgot to do so.

In my frustration, I ran out of the house but forgot that the screen door had been recently replaced by a glass door. My right hand broke through the glass and caused a big gash. Blood spurted everywhere.

Dad called 911, and paramedics rushed me to the hospital. Along the way, Dad — who was accompanying me in the ambulance, stroked my hair and told me that he loved me.

I momentarily forgot the excruciating pain I was in. *My*

father was telling me that he loved me? I couldn't recall hearing him say that before.

When we arrived at the emergency room, it took forty stitches to stop the heavy bleeding. The ER doc said it looked like I was one of the lucky ones—I should fully recover, he said.

I breathed a heavy sigh of relief because I was starting to play tennis in high school. This would have been around 1970, when tennis was becoming popular after the game opened up to professionals in 1968. I would drive to Canton to some public courts and pick up games. The same old crowd played there, and everyone looked after each other. This Jewish man named Ben saw me play one time and called me over when I was done.

"Tell you what, kid," Ben said. "I'll play with you until you can beat me three times. Then you're on your own."

I looked at this older man. I was sure I could outhit him. I didn't see how he could beat me. I knew I had the game to beat Ben, and I could run all day.

"Okay, let's play tomorrow," I said.

During the warm-up, I thought I could overpower Ben, who seemed to put nothing on the ball. That day, however, he beat me handily. How did he do that? Because he had better control. He moved me around the court like I was on the end of a windshield wiper. I was so tired from running side-to-side and chasing after his well-placed shots that I promised myself that he'd never beat me again.

But things didn't happen that way. Ben dusted me several more times until I figured out that I needed to take some speed off my hits and play steadier instead of going for low percentage winners. It wasn't long before my new "control" game got the better of Ben, and I beat him three times in a row. True to his word, he stopped playing me.

My high school didn't have a tennis team, so I just played local tennis tournaments, mainly in Canton. I wasn't thinking about going to college or playing on a college tennis team. Truth be known, I wasn't a very good student. My below-average report card was littered with Cs and Ds. I didn't apply myself to schoolwork, especially after I got my Ford Mustang. Though I wasn't much of a student, I did like my extracurricular activities, which was being the sports editor of the school newspaper and being involved in the drama club. We did two plays a year, and I was in every one of them. My biggest role was in *The Music Man*, where I was part of the barbershop quartet.

I received my most support from my journalism teacher, Mrs. Stevenson, who took an interest in me. She wanted me to go to college, but I wasn't so sure I was cut out for a four-year degree.

Mrs. Stevenson told me I was being obstinate and even went to the trouble of arranging an interview for me at Malone College in nearby Canton. She also knew of my tennis interest, so she asked the Malone tennis coaches, Glenn Lipley and Burley Smith, if they would interview me as well. Both coaches asked me to come out for the tennis team, and they even offered me a scholarship to play tennis—$50.

Fifty dollars wasn't much, just book money, but the fact that *somebody* wanted me to play my favorite sport was enough to get me to attend Malone College. I barely made the starting team my freshman year, though, playing No. 6, but the upgrade in competition raised my game. I played a lot of tournaments over the summer, and when I came back for my sophomore year, I moved up the ladder to No. 3 and then No. 2 for my junior and senior years. I also played No.

MALONE UNIVERSITY

CHRIST'S KINGDOM FIRST

FRITZ GLAUS
Class of 1976
Men's Tennis

Malone graduate, was a four-year letterman on the Pioneer tennis team. Glaus, who did not begin playing tennis until just one year prior to coming to Malone, became the team's number one singles and doubles player for both the 1975 and 1976 seasons. He was the Most Valuable Player on the '75 squad and helped the '76 team qualify for the NAIA National Tournament. Upon graduating from Malone, Glaus traveled the world for 20 years teaching and playing tennis and, in addition, was a chaplain on the men's professional tour for 11 years.

One of the great honors of my life was being inducted into the Sports Hall of Fame of my alma mater, Malone College, in 1998. I was overwhelmed with the love that was shown me when I arrived on campus for the ceremony. What an awesome day that was—go Pioneers!

1 doubles with Chris Ramsburg. We had a very good team, and being part of a team with a bunch of guys I liked was tons of fun.

I also liked the camaraderie of being part of the drama club. In my junior year, I won the lead role in our production of *Blithe Spirit,* a comic play by Noel Coward about a socialist/novelist who can "hear" the ghost of his first wife but his second wife, Ruth, cannot.

During the play's run, I was in Findlay, Ohio, playing a team match and didn't get back to the college until ten minutes before the opening act. When the curtain went up, I forgot all my lines because I was still in tennis mode. Everyone picked up the slack, and I eventually remembered what I was supposed to say.

There was another incident during my junior year that remains an indelible memory. A friend, Pam Mason, called me one night around 1 a.m. and asked if I could walk around the track with her. Going for a walk in the middle of the night was a typical crazy college thing to do, but I was game.

As we walked around the track on that moonlit night, she stopped and pointed toward the city lights of Canton.

"You see the lights of the city?" she asked.

"Sure," I replied. "They're pretty."

"I feel like the Lord is telling me that you will see the lights of the world some day."

"That's nice," I said, but what Pam said didn't register with me. Except for the long trip from Switzerland when I was two years old—which I couldn't remember—I had stayed put in the Ohio Valley. The furthest I had ever been from home was a hundred miles or so.

Little did I know that Pam would be right.

Going Forward

My parents didn't take me to church much when I was growing up.

We were Christmas-and-Easter churchgoers at a local Methodist church. Mom and Dad had a typical European attitude about church, which was that it was a place where you got married, had your kids baptized, and gathered for funerals. Otherwise, church wasn't important.

During my junior year at Malone College, Pam Mason and several other friends invited me to see a Billy Graham movie called *Time to Run*, a film about a young runaway named Barbara who's mad at the world and skeptical of all the claims of Christianity. By the end of movie, Barbara realizes that she's been running away from God, and when she hears we are all sinful and separated from Him, she gives her life to Jesus Christ so she can know and experience God's love and plan for her life.

Sure, the movie was formulaic, but to a twenty-one-year-old kid trying to figure out a crazy world, everything made sense. I had a hole in my heart, and only Jesus could fill it.

When the film was over, a local preacher explained the gospel in greater detail, saying that I could have eternal life with Jesus Christ if only I would believe in Him. He walked us through the "Roman road," quoting from the Book of Romans that we have "all sinned and fallen short of the glory of God" (Romans 3:23), and the problem we all face us is that the "wages of sin is death" (Romans 6:23). But the second part of that verse says that the "free gift of God is eternal life through Jesus Christ."

The preacher then quoted Romans 10:9, saying, "If you will confess with your mouth that Jesus Christ is Lord, and shall believe in your heart that God has raised Him from the dead, you shall be saved."

I felt God tugging at my heart like I had never felt before, and when people were invited to "come forward" and make a public demonstration of their new faith in Jesus Christ, I stood up and slowly walked to the front of the auditorium, where somebody prayed with me.

My life changed that night. I became a follower of Christ. I didn't care who knew. I belonged to Jesus Christ now. I started attending an evangelical church on campus and also weekly Bible studies. My faith was important to me and gave me a purpose.

Something else changed about me after that evening—I became a good student. All of a sudden, my life meant something, and that meant I needed to buckle down on my schoolwork because I was responsible before God to do the best I could do. From midway through my junior year until I graduated, I made honor roll every semester.

During the summer before my senior year, I was playing a United States Tennis Association (USTA) tournament in Cleveland. After my match, a man walked up to me and said that I would be a good person to work for Peter Burwash International, a tennis management company that provided teaching pros for resorts and tennis clubs around the world. The company had been founded a few years earlier by a former Canadian player named Peter Burwash, said the fellow. He handed me some literature that described Peter Burwash International (PBI) as "the world's first international group of tennis coaches whose principal function is to staff quality resorts, hotels, tennis clubs, and camps with locations in Hawaii, California, the South Pacific, the Caribbean, Canada, Europe, and Asia."

"You're just the kind of person we're looking for at Peter

Burwash International," the recruiter said. "Think about it." He handed me his card, and I gave him my address and phone number.

I hadn't thought much about what I wanted to do after I graduated from college. One thing I knew is that I didn't want to work at Nickles baking bread and hot dog buns.

Sometime during my senior tennis season in the spring of 1976, I got a phone call from someone with Peter Burwash International, asking me if I wanted to come to Chicago for an interview.

My excitement level rose. "That sounds great," I replied. Here was a chance to see the world. Heck, here was a chance to take my first plane flight.

The meeting was held at a hotel near the O'Hare Airport, and Peter Burwash himself conducted the interview. Dressed in stylish tennis whites, he walked into the conference room carrying ten rackets for some reason. He looked to be around thirty years old, tanned, extremely fit. He flashed a big smile and thrust out a hand in greeting. He struck me as one charismatic dude.

He didn't seem to be that interested in my tennis, though. Instead, Peter bore in and asked me several open-ended questions about my personal life, such as *Is there some area of your life that you would like to improve?*

No, I replied. Life was good. I had just come off a great senior season, winning a lot of matches and helping my team qualify for the NCAA Division III championships. I had a college degree in hand, and my entire future was ahead of me.

Then Peter asked me what I thought about religion. I shrugged my shoulders and told him that I believed in Jesus Christ and knew that He had a plan for my life.

I departed the interview not sure of what to make of my time with Peter Burwash inside the hotel conference room. I couldn't tell if I had made a good impression or given Peter the answers he was looking for.

Nevertheless, three weeks later I received a letter from Peter Burwash International offering me a position as a tennis teacher. Since I didn't have any other strong job prospects, was footloose and fancy free, and viewed this as a chance to see the world, I leaped at the opportunity. First, however, I would have to go through a training session held at Parry Sound north of Toronto, Canada, led by none other than Peter Burwash.

There were probably twenty-five aspiring pros just as eager as I was to teach tennis someplace in this world. I soon learned that we were all there to learn the Peter Burwash way of teaching tennis, which made a certain amount of sense. He couldn't have hundreds of teaching pros around the world doing their own thing on the court. There had to be some sort of quality control.

We were told that we were not teaching a certain "method" because "we teach individuals, not systems." Nonetheless, we were given our share of do's and don'ts. I had to change my grip—which was a continental grip—and use their Eastern grips on the forehand and backhand. Those changes took a couple of days of getting used, but all was good. We were also taught a variety of drills to use in private and group lessons, which gave me confidence that I could give a good lesson.

Off to the Islands

During our training, we were asked to select resort hotels or regions of the world where we would like to teach. I think

I checked the box next to "Hawaii" three times. For someone who had never visited the Atlantic or Pacific Ocean, Hawaii sounded as exotic as they come.

Just before the three-day training session was over, Peter called me into his office.

"I see that you'd like to go to Hawaii," he began."

"Hawaii sounds great to me," I replied.

"I'll send you to Hawaii, but you'll have to do one thing for me."

"What's that?"

"Become a vegetarian."

A vegetarian? I wasn't sure why he asked me not to eat meat any more, but I wanted to go to Hawaii so badly that I quickly said yes to becoming a vegetarian. They had a lot of sweet fruits like papaya and pineapple in Hawaii, right?

Upon my arrival in Honolulu, I was driven to Peter Burwash International headquarters in Honolulu, where I would live and sleep in dorm rooms. My first assignment to teach tennis at Hickman Air Force Base next to Pearl Harbor, giving lessons to the children of military families as well as group classes for the adults. I was a happy camper and loved everything about Oahu: the soft tropical breezes, the sandy beaches, the bathtub-warm water, and even the late-after-noon rain showers. Hawaii was magical, just what I'd pictured it would be.

I soon found out why Peter asked me to become a vegetarian. There were several other PBI pros staying in the dorms, and each morning at 4 a.m., I could hear them chanting words that sounded like the end of the George Harrison song, "My Sweet Lord." You know, *Krishna, Krishna, hare, hare, guru Vishnu, maheshara, guru sakshaat, hare rama.*

My fellow pros were Hare Krishnas, and that's why they

didn't eat meat. They were Hare Krishnas because Peter Burwash was a Hare Krishna and had introduced them to the religion.

During my time in Hawaii, however, there was no effort made to convert me, but I would always hear them chant long before dawn. I asked one time why they chanted at 4 a.m., and I was told that God listens best at four o'clock in the morning. I also was told that Hare Krishnas usually have ponytails because they believe that's the way God will pull them up to heaven. None of the Peter Burwash pros, nor Peter, wore ponytails, however, even though the Hare Krishnas I saw handing out roses and tracts at the airport in their flowing robes all had ponytails.

I soon figured out that Peter Burwash liked to hire young men who were religious minded or professed to be Christians: he believed sooner or later that they would want to become Hare Krishnas after seeing how he and his fellow Hare Krishnas lived. Because of this, I sensed I needed to find a solid Bible-based church soon, and I found some great fellowship at an Assembly of God church in Honolulu.

Meanwhile, days were long on the tennis court. It wasn't unusual for us to be teaching from 8 a.m. to 7 p.m. at night with a couple of hours off for lunch or afternoon break. Only young people in their twenties have the stamina to be out on the court that long, but I did my best to make tennis fun for my students as well as for me.

I must have done good work because after three months at Hickam, PBI sent me to the Hilton Hotel on Oahu's North Shore as the new tennis director. I met a surfboard maker, Bill Barnfield, and his wife, Wendy, and they enthusiastically told me about North Shore Christian Fellowship, so I hooked up with them. I was given a great room at the Hilton that overlooked the ocean, and I can still remember reading my Bible and looking at the azure blue water in the distance, amazed at the beauty of God's creation.

My next assignment was on the island of Kauai at the Kiahuna Tennis Club. I came in as the tennis director, and my assistant director was a Mormon and the other pro was a Christian Science adherent. (I told you that Peter Burwash liked to hire those with a religious bent.) We had a sign that said, "Play a pro. If he beats you, you owe $10. If you win, you owe nothing."

I remember the time a guy in the latest tennis duds came to challenge me, and I beat him pretty easily for my $10. Then a guy with a ragged, dirty tennis outfit approached me, carrying a single racket. I didn't win a game. Turns out he was part of the Hungarian Davis Cup team in Hawaii on holiday.

Although I was spending most of my waking hours at the Kiahuna Tennis Club, I did get involved in the local community by trying out for a play called *The Drunkard*. I won the lead role in this melodrama where you could talk to the audience but the other actors on the stage couldn't hear you. The plotline was that an evil person in the village wanted my wife, so we made up a story that I was drunkard, which people believed until everything was revealed in the end.

After six months in Kauai—and a short stint in Hong Kong, which was fascinating—Peter called and said that a PBI teaching pro from Canada was supposed to go to the Fiji Islands, but he did not have his visa. Did I want to go in his place?

I had a visa, since I was in Hong Kong, so I hopped on a flight for Fiji, proud of the knowledge that I would be the first teaching pro from outside Fiji to teach tennis at the Regent of Fiji Hotel on Denarau Island. What untouched

Back home in Brewster, Ohio, the local newspaper published
a feature about me teaching tennis in the Fiji Islands.

beauty! Fiji was amazing, and you could pick just about any
one of their 300 islands and be the only person there.

This time around I mainly taught tourists, who came primarily from New Zealand and Australia. It didn't hurt matters that they had several grass courts, which were wonderful to teach and play on. With the thatched roofs, Tiki motif,
and the pink skies at sunset, this was Bali Hai.

I found a nice Christian church and met some Hindus
who asked questions about my faith. I shared the gospel with
them, and they became Christians. I had lots of experiences
like that. One time I was eating alone in the hotel restaurant

when a young woman named Claudia came over to my table and asked if I was the tennis pro. I said yes and invited her to sit down, and before long, we started talking about Christ and she accepted the Lord that day. She was like an apple waiting to fall off the tree.

Those were the first times I shared the gospel and led people into a relationship with Christ. I liked the feeling that God could use me anywhere—even halfway across the world from my hometown, twelve time zones away across the International Date Line. I remember sharing my faith with my assistant pro, who was Thai and had taught himself to teach tennis despite losing his left arm when he was hit by a bus years earlier. He thought that terrible accident happened to him because he had done something bad in his previous life, but I told him he didn't have a previous life because the God of the Bible, through Jesus Christ, created each and everyone of us.

My two best friends in Fiji were Robert Patel and Shantal Fal, who were both from India. In fact, a lot of people from Fiji have Indian ancestry—like golfer Vijay Singh.

Robert and Shantal weren't golfers but avid tennis players. I'll never forget the time when Robert invited me to his wedding. I casually asked him if he had met his bride yet, and he smiled and said no. His parents had picked out the girl for him, which seemed unfathomable to me.

I met some interesting people in Fiji. One was actor Lloyd Bridges, father of Hollywood stars Beau Bridges and Jeff Bridges. He was a guest at the hotel, so we played some. Then Lloyd invited me and several colleagues to go scuba diving with him, which was a kick because I had grown up watching him play the role of ex-Navy frogman Mike Nelson in *Sea Hunt*.

Lloyd was especially friendly, and when he heard that we were holding a fund-raiser for Jim Noble, a PBI tennis pro in the Caribbean who had cancer, the actor agreed to play an exhibition match with me. At that time, fifty West Virginia miners were staying at the hotel, but they couldn't leave the island because the local airport was on strike. When they passed the hat, the coal miners gave us $1,600 to help out Jim Noble.

Another time, a good-looking guy in his late forties asked me to play with him. With an Aussie accent, he introduced himself as Malcolm Fraser. I shook his hand and said I was Fritz Glaus, and we made a date for the following morning. When he left the court, I noticed two nervous men in business suits—rare for a setting like Fiji—following closely behind.

I didn't think anything of it until Malcolm returned the following morning, dressed in tennis whites, carrying a couple of rackets, and trailed by the same two guys wearing suits and dark sunglasses.

I grabbed my bucket of balls and started feeding him. I like to keep up a chatter when I give a lesson, so after I had moved him around a bit and winded him, I asked Malcolm what he did.

"I'm the Prime Minister of Australia," he said.

I wasn't sure what he meant, so I asked him what a prime minister was.

"It's the same as being President of your United States," he said.

I apologized for being clueless, but that explained why bodyguards were always around him—even on a remote island in the middle of the South Pacific. That also explained why I saw pistols in leather holsters whenever his bodyguards bent over to pick up balls with us at the end of the lesson.

The Prime Minister was interested in getting a good workout, so I made sure I moved him around and let him enjoy a respite from the cares of running Australia. Turns out that Malcolm Fraser was Prime Minister from 1975 to 1983.

Thai Food

After six months in Fiji, Peter sent me to a resort hotel in Thailand — the Hotel Siam Bayshore. Keep in mind that this was in 1977, long before Thailand became a popular tourist destination for Americans. One of the first resort areas was Pattaya Beach in the Gulf of Thailand — more than 600 miles northeast of popular Phuket, which is situated on the Indian Ocean and was the site of the horrific tsunami in 2004.

The first thing I did when I went to Pattaya Beach was look for Christian fellowship. I thought I was a long way from home in Fiji; now I was *really* a long way from the heartland. I asked around, saying I was looking for a Christian church or a missionary family nearby. I found such a family — Duane and Betty Kleple with the Assembly of God Missionary Alliance — who welcomed me. We would spend a lot of time together, and before I left Southeast Asia Duane would baptize me in the Gulf of Thailand.

The owner of the Siam Bayshore was a Thai woman who married an American named Terry who took me under his wing a bit and explained how things went down in Thailand. One thing we talked about was the sex trade, which was a flourishing business, even back in the 1970s. Prostitutes were everywhere in Thailand, standing on street corners or waiting outside the arrival lounge at the airports. I saw a lot of older European men — usually Germans — arriving in the country with one thing on their mind. They called it "sex tourism."

I quickly learned my first phrase in the Thai language — *Mâi ao khàp khun* — which meant "No thank you." That's what I had to say each time I was propositioned in downtown Pattaya Beach, which had a teeming population of more than 500,000. They soon got the hint that I wasn't interested in them.

I certainly felt sorry for the Thai prostitutes, however. Uniformly young, often under the age of sixteen, many were shanghaied into sex slavery. Others sold their bodies because they could make more money doing sexual favors than anything else.

I'll never forget the time I accompanied Duane and Betty for the arrival of the USS Kitty Hawk, the American carrier. As the giddy sailors disembarked for shore leave, we held up

The Kleple family welcomed me after I arrived in Thailand.

a huge plasterboard sign that said CHRISTIAN FELLOW-SHIP. Next to us, however, was a flat-bed truck filled with a couple of dozen prostitutes, all giving come-hither looks and waving at the sailors to come on over.

The choice was stark, but we had many U.S. sailors join us for Christian fun and fellowship. One night, I befriended a sailor who looked down and out. Thinking he was homesick, I asked him why he looked so discouraged. "Because my buddy is out with some hooker," he said.

I asked him why he wasn't doing the same thing, and he replied, "I just can't. I'm a slave to righteousness."

On my one day off a week I liked to rent a motorcycle and ride out into the countryside and hand out Christian tracts to the kids I ran into in the small towns I passed through. I would also visit Dr. Alton Hood, a Baptist medical missionary, at his compound. He was a happy, colorful physician who liked to joke that he was "busier than a one-armed paper hanger" because the medical needs were so great.

One time I saw him do several surgeries and was paid the equivalent of five U.S. dollars in the local currency. In America, he would have been a millionaire, but by devoting his life to the service of others in the mission field, he stored up riches in heaven. Dr. Hood greatly inspired me, and sometimes when I had an entire weekend off, I would stay two days and teach the missionary kids how to play tennis.

On another motorcycle trip, I traveled to northern Thailand where I visited a leprosy camp that was part of a Christian outreach. Seeing how those with leprosy—a chronic bacterial disease of the skin and nerves in the hands and feet—were treated with respect by the Christian aid workers moved me.

Thailand was full of rich experiences for me, including

the time when a missionary family and I taught Buddhist monks English—using the Bible as our textbook. That prompted an invitation to witness the graduation of several Buddhist monks. While sitting there, I crossed my leg and put my right foot on top of my left knee. That's a no-no in Thai culture because you're not supposed to show people the sole of your foot. An exasperated monk reached over and wordlessly put my right foot back on the ground. I wanted to crawl into a hole for committing the social faux pas.

Then there was the American dentist who took some lessons from me. We did a trade-out: I'd teach him tennis and he'd clean my teeth and fill any cavities. We got to know each so well that he confided that he was also a CIA agent. He had been recruited back in dental school when he was asked if he would like to travel and see the world.

Sound familiar?

When he said yes, the CIA trained him as an agent and stationed him in Pattaya Beach. His job was to keep Communists out of Thailand. If they caught operatives, at first he would send them back. If he caught them a second time, they were jailed. If they caught them a third time, they would be killed. He was serious.

Thailand opened my eyes to the reality of the world and gave me experiences that would come in handy when I became a chaplain on the pro tennis tour.

The Sound of Music

After six months in Thailand, I heard from Peter. I had a new assignment, he said in his typical brisk manner. He said I was going to Going.

I thought he was playing some Abbot and Costello trick on me, but Peter was serious: my next port of call would be

Going, Austria, located in the Tyrolean Alps.

"How's your German?" he asked.

"Nicht so gut," I responded. I had learned a mishmash of Swiss-German and German from the parents, which are actually two different languages. Germans can't understand Swiss-German but Swiss can understand and speak to Germans because they learn High German in school from a young age.

Before I left Thailand, I gave free lessons to any German who would teach me German during the lesson and sit down with me afterward for a tutorial. I wanted to be able to speak at last some German when I arrived in Austria.

Before I started in Austria, I attended the annual Peter Burwash International held in Hawaii. Peter approached me and said that since I was a Christian, I could share my faith to anyone who wanted to come hear me talk. While that happened, he would speak about Hara Krishna in another room to anyone who wanted to hear him speak on that topic.

That sounded reasonable and fine, and I was excited to share my faith with some of the other PBI pros. When I started to share my testimony, however, a handful of the PBI pros who were Hara Krishnas disrupted our meeting and didn't let me speak, shouting to keep me from being heard.

"Let Fritz talk!" yelled out one pro in the back.

Eventually, things quieted down and I was able to share my journey and how Christ died on the cross and was resurrected from the dead so that we might have eternal life. I thought it was great that Peter allowed me to do that.

The Burwash organization had a system of "ranking" their tennis pros that was based on tangible things like seniority and teaching ability and intangible criteria—like if you were Hara Krishna. By this time, I had worked myself up to

No. 13 in the organization (out of probably thirty-five tennis pros), but everyone ahead of me was a Hara Krishna.

Even though I felt like the odd man out sometimes, I was excited about my new summer assignment in Austria. I don't know if that was my Swiss heritage coming to the surface, but it felt like I was going back to the old country. My German got better each day, and I got bolder in my faith: I shared Christ with many of the Austrians, Germans, and Swiss who came to our one-week tennis camps. In the evenings, I mingled with our campers and even learned to yodel with a couple of cute Austrian girls dressed in dirndls.

Our camps were always full, and we taught six days a week. If we wanted to pick up some extra money, we could teach after our eight-hour day was done. I can remember giving a half-dozen lessons to Austrian ski hero Franz Klammer, who a year and a half earlier had won the gold medal at the 1976 Innsbruck Olympics, nearly crashing several times down a scary downhill course.

On Sundays, the last place I wanted to be was on a tennis court, so what I'd do was jump on a train to Salzburg, where I attended an evangelical or "free" church. I found it wonderful to meet Christians from all over the world.

When the summer was over, we taught inside a tennis *Halle* with carpet for courts. I learned to ski, so that was fun. I became friends with a local Austrian family who had a daughter name Binya. She was an acrobat on skis and in shows around Europe. The family had me over to their house many times to eat Wienerschnitzel and goulash.

One time, several of my Swiss cousins surprised me by picking me up and taking me back to Switzerland to meet all my relatives. I had called them a few months earlier and told them where I was. They arranged things with PBI to take me

Could my tennis shorts get any shorter? That was the style
back in the late 1970s. Here I'm featured on the cover
of an Austrian tennis magazine.

I taught tennis under the snow-capped Austrian Alps and had a lot of great times during my time in the Tyrol.

away for a few days.

The first place I stayed was just outside of Interlaken in the heart of William Tell country. Then my Aunt Sophie Grüson and her husband, Fritz, invited me to stay at their home in Frutigen, a picturesque village of 5,000 at the base of the Bernese Oberland. Most Swiss homes have the name of the person who built the place, a tradition that was centuries old. I couldn't help but noticed that Fritz and Sophie's house had the words *Jesus Christ* etched in the stone above their front door.

When I asked her in my American-accented German why Jesus' name was there, she said it was because the Lord built their house. I took that opportunity to tell Sophie that I was a Christian, which unleashed a torrent of tears.

"I prayed for you when you were one hour old that you'd become a Christian," she said, dabbing at tears with her embroidered handkerchief. We must have hugged each other for an hour.

While in Switzerland, I added a side trip to Lausanne—in the French-speaking side of Switzerland—to visit Sylvia Bachman, a full-time staff member with Youth for a Mission, an international, inter-denominational missionary organization. She wanted to meet me after several YWAM youth missionaries spent some with me in Fiji, and I fellowshipped with them.

We exchanged pleasantries, and then she casually asked if I wanted to play some tennis with a local family. They had a nice home, she said, with two tennis clay tennis courts on their property.

I don't know what you would call the home of Henri Andre and his family—a stately manor, countryside villa, or a handsome mansion, but I could get used to a place like this.

Henri was French, but he spoke good German and English. He had made his money building hospitals and rest homes.

I enjoyed playing some casual tennis with Henri and his family, who were keen on the game. Afterward, while sipping lemonade on the veranda, Henri mentioned that he had a friend coming from the States. In fact, he just landed at the Geneva Airport and would be there in an hour.

"I'd like you to meet him," Henri said.

"And who would that be?" I asked.

"Eddie Waxer."

I had heard that name before. Little did I know that our introduction in Switzerland would set me a course to become a chaplain on the men's professional tennis tour.

With my Aunt Sophie in her hometown of Frutigen, Switzerland.

Eddie Waxer, who's devoted his life to sports evangelism, is the person responsible for me becoming a chaplain on the professional tennis tour.

2

THE START OF THE TENNIS MINISTRY

Eddie Waxer was someone who had been involved in sports ministry for nearly a decade. He had a well-deserved reputation for being a master at bringing together leaders and organizations to partner on global sports evangelism.

I first heard Eddie's name six months earlier when I was back in the States, and how that happened is an interesting story that shows how the hand of God can work. The story begins when Brenda Brenneman, the Resident Counselor for Women at Malone College, attended a Young Life conference in the Midwest where she heard youth speaker Milt Richards deliver an inspirational address. Brenda and I had gotten to know each other when I was a member of the resident hall staff.

At this Young Life conference, Milt talked about his love for tennis and how he was working with Stan Smith on some outreach events. Stan was well known in the tennis world because he had reached No. 1 in the world after winning the U.S. Open in 1971 and Wimbledon in 1972.

Brenda, sitting in the audience, knew someone else who loved tennis—me! She approached Milt afterward and said there was a young man teaching tennis for an organization with a strong Eastern religion bent who wanted to get into full-time Christian ministry at some point. She said that she had seen me frequently on my return trips home and had witnessed great spiritual growth. My exposure to a wide range of cultures, different religions, and Christians living out their faith in a dozen countries had to count for something, she said. Brenda noted that I openly shared Christ with people in airports and players on the tennis court.

In a follow-up letter, Brenda wrote, "Milt, I don't know what you may have in the works with Stan Smith, but I just feel led to bring Fritz Glaus to your attention and see what may develop. I'm sure you've seen many times how a person's background can be preparation for ministry, and it seems like all his travel and experiences are for a specific reason in Fritz's life." Brenda then included my overseas address.

Milt acted upon that letter and contacted me. He asked me to come to Washington, D.C. for an outreach event involving golf and tennis. Larry Nelson, the winner of the 1983 U.S. Open championship, was conducting a golf clinic, and Stan Smith was in charge of the tennis side. Stan could use some help, he said, which is where I came in. Since this sounded like a great opportunity to meet one of my tennis heroes—and the timing worked out for me to be back in the States—I immediately said yes.

When I arrived at the country club outside our nation's capitol, I asked Milt why he asked me to help out—since there were dozens of other pros he could have called upon. "I enjoy bringing like-minded people together to see what might happen," he replied.

Conducting a clinic with Stan was a wonderful experi-ence, and that night the former No. 1 player and I talked for several hours about the need for a professional tennis min-istry. He said the person I needed to meet one day was Eddie Waxer. I filed that name away in my memory bank.

And now I was about to meet Eddie at a palatial estate along the Lake of Geneva — the Swiss Riviera. Following our casual match, Henri invited me to sip lemonade on the veranda until Eddie's arrival.

Even though Eddie was a bit jet-lagged from his long trip across the Pond, he listened intently as I described the jour-ney I had been on: playing tennis at Malone College; joining Peter Burwash International following graduation; teaching tennis in beautiful resort settings around the world; and meeting thousands of interesting people. "Sometimes I feel more like a missionary than a tennis instructor," I said. This was due to my efforts to be salt and light with PBI as well as a Christian witness to those whom I came into contact with in far-flung countries that rarely heard the Good News of God's love.

"That's why you should think about being part of a ten-nis ministry," he said.

"But I have no training —"

Eddie stopped me. "What I'm thinking is that maybe God has been preparing you for a special time like this. There's a real need for someone to travel on the professional tennis tour to disciple the players and lead others to Christ."

"Isn't someone doing that now?" I asked. I figured that professional tennis already had a tour chaplain, much like the chaplains I heard about for major league baseball teams and the NFL.

Eddie said that wasn't the case with tennis. In the early 1970s, Eddie said he had traveled to a few tournaments at the request of Stan Smith, a player he had befriended and who took his faith seriously. But it was a hit-and-miss effort because he oversaw evangelism ministries in other sports, like golf and motor car racing.

What Eddie was mainly doing back then was developing — actually, inventing — sports ministry for Athletes in Action, which was part of the Campus Crusade for Christ ministry. Since he had a lot on his plate, he asked Ramsey Earnhardt, a former top amateur player from the early 1960s, to travel a bit with the tour, offering chapel services for the players. That ended after a couple of years, Eddie said, because Ramsey was married with a family and didn't want to be away from home that much. Now, with tennis rapidly rising in popularity in the late 1970s, there was thought of sending another tennis chaplain out on the tour. That person could be me. Eddie asked me to pray about it.

I told him I would, but we both agreed that I would need to return to school and get some training to deepen my knowledge of the Bible first.

Eddie and I exchanged several more letters after I returned to Austria, urging me to consider where God was leading me. He certainly gave me a lot to think about. For the better part of a year, I felt like my time with Peter Burwash International was coming to an end, causing me to wonder if God was opening the door to a full-time ministry in tennis. I decided to step out in faith and make plans to attend an evangelical Bible school in Austria that was part of InterVarsity Press. I figured that was a good place to start.

Before I enrolled, however, I made a trip to the United States and visited a friend of mine, Rob Reichel, at Hilton

Head Island, South Carolina. While there, I was asked to hit some balls with an Atlanta pastor named Randy Pope. We had a spirited game, and afterward we sat down to chat.

"What do you see yourself doing in ten years?" he asked.

That was easy. "I want to have a ministry in tennis," I replied, and then I told him about my plans to study the Bible and receive missionary training in Austria with an eye toward helping Eddie Waxer and his outreach to the professional tennis tour.

"You should go to a seminary here in the U.S.," Randy said. I was intrigued by his idea, so we talked about what that would look like.

Long story short, when I left Peter Burwash International, I moved to Dallas, where I enrolled at the Center for Advanced Biblical Studies. Their two-year program was a wonderful experience. As part of my post-graduate degree, I had to have a ministry of my own, so I started a Bible study at a tennis club.

During that time, a friend invited me to a meeting at T Bar M Ranch near San Antonio, Texas. Actually it wasn't a meeting but a mini-convention comprised of people representing every professional sport in America. The goal was how to reach out and disciple athletes for Christ.

Eddie Waxer was there. He had asked five professional tennis players to come to T Bar M to talk about resurrecting the idea of having a chaplain follow the tour and be available to the players. The five professional players were Stan Smith, brothers Sandy and Gene Mayer, Mike Cahill, and Terry Moor.

And that's when I was asked to become their tennis chaplain. The five players said they would financially support me, and Eddie Waxer also promised that he would find other financial angels to keep me traveling on the tour. A church, The Chapel in Akron, Ohio, would be my home church, and Hal Schaus of The Chapel would head up my accountability group. We all agreed that it would be important that the tennis ministry be anchored to a solid, Bible-teaching church, where I would be a full-fledged staff member and would have a place to go when I wasn't traveling.

I was ready. I was single, had traveled the world, had an international outlook, and had nothing in my life holding me back.

Eddie was thrilled that I said yes, but he had some advice that he wanted to impart. "The world of sports is dominated by egos," he said. "It's very important that the athletes don't feel like you're using them. Do not ask the players for any rackets, clothes, or tickets," he said. "Do not ask them for anything, not even to have your picture taken with them. You are there to be their servant." He warned me to restrain from creating expectations that the players should pay for my meals and reminded me to always have an attitude of being in a servant's role.

Eddie also recommended that I not give myself a fancy title, like "Director of Sports Ministries" or something of that sort, but that introducing myself as a "chaplain" or "minister" would suffice.

Eddie and I then drew up a list of my responsibilities, which could be boiled down to the following points:
- Disciple existing Christian players on the men's tour
- Follow up with new Christians on the tour
- Make myself available to a growing number of players who express an interest in spiritual matters
- Continue to cultivate relationships with non-Christian players

• Identify key Christian leaders in the international tennis community who could speak to players about Christ in their mother tongue

• Recognize spiritual needs and explore ministry opportunities worldwide

During my time as a tennis chaplain, the number of players who expressed an interest in spiritual matters surprised me. You name a famous player from the 1980s to early 1990s, and nearly all talked to me at one time or another. It never ceased to amaze me how these top players—who were paid millions of dollars, fawned over by the media, worshipped by fans, and could have pretty much anything they wanted, including women—knew that deep down they were still missing something.

Too many thought, however, that they would lose something when they turned to Christ when it was the other way around.

Following the Tour

I began traveling on the men's ATP Tour in February 1980, and during the first year, I was introduced as Stan Smith's friend, which was a nice calling card to have and gave me instant credibility. I either stayed in the player's hotels or was invited to stay in the homes of Christian families.

Back in 1980, the players probably made a tenth of what they make now in tournament prize money. That would all change, but at the start of the 1980s, most players weren't staying in five-star hotels. Those ranked outside the Top 50 often looked to cut expenses by staying in "housing" provided by generous families who opened up their homes to the players on behalf of the tournament. That's what I did to stretch my budget as well.

I soon found out that part of my job description included matching Christian families with either Christian players or any player, for that matter, who needed a place to stay during the tournament. Eddie Waxer had a global network that was amazing. I witnessed the players and their host families bond in incredible ways, and many returned the following year to stay with the same family. Working out the housing arrangements turned out to be one of those enriching experiences for *everyone* — the host families as well as the touring pros, who were glad to get some home-cooked meals and TLC.

One time I got a phone call from the head coach at Georgia Tech, Gary Niebur, who told me that a couple of his players, Bryan Shelton and Kenny Thorne, were graduating in June and turning pro. They needed housing for a series of summer tournaments in Germany. Could I help them?

I said sure. My first phone call was to Eddie Waxer, who gave me a contact person with Sportler-ruft-Sportler, a German Christian sports organization similar to Athletes in Action in the States. They saw the ministry value in matching up players with Christian families.

I explained the situation to a secretary and gave her their arrival and departure dates. She took down all the information and said she'd organize a family at every tour stop. All these Americans had to do was call her upon their arrival in Stuttgart and let her know their train itinerary for their first tournament. She would have a family waiting when the train rolled in.

Everything worked with Teutonic precision, and Bryan and Kenny had an awesome experience. The host family was waiting on the train platform, the beds were comfortable, the

German food was good, and the players had an instant cheering section. They made deep friendships that have lasted to this day.

At the end of the tour, I received thank you letters from Bryan and Kenny's parents, thanking me for organizing the housing. This was their sons' first trip to Europe, they said, and it couldn't have gone better. It helped that both Bryan and Kenny were solid, mature believers raised in loving Christian homes. In years to come, they would be the ones I could count on to attend the weekly Bible studies I hosted.

Sometimes procuring housing didn't go so smoothly. Believe me, the logistics weren't easy before smartphones and GPS apps. Organizing housing was quite a coordination hassle in those days, relying on surface mail and phone calls to homes and businesses. I haven't forgotten all the times when I had to go find the local post office, where they had phone booths and much better rates than the pay phones next to a busy shopping district. It helped that I had access to an international phone card donated by a Christian businessman who loved tennis and believed in what I was doing.

The two most important tournaments for housing were the French Open and Wimbledon, two-week tournaments in two of the most expensive cities in the world: Paris and London. For Roland Garros, we worked through an American missionary in Paris named Mr. Dodd, and he always did a great job setting up housing for the men and women.

At Wimbledon, Mark and Iona Birchall arranged housing with Christian families and opened their home as a center for Bible studies and times of fellowship. They found housing for more than a dozen players, and the bonds between the host families and the players became so strong that the play-

Iona Birchall (left) opened her home for Bible studies and fellowship during Wimbledon every summer.

ers *wanted* to stay with the same families every year.

One year, the Birchalls hosted a garden party in their expansive back yard. Around fifty people were there—players, host families, and a handful of invited guests.

One of their guests thrust out his hand in greeting. "I'm Cliff Richard," he said.

He was a good-looking chap, early forties, dressed fashionably, and carried himself well.

"Fritz Glaus," I replied, shaking his hand. "What do you do?"

"I sing." Cliff Richard flashed a friendly grin.

"Really? I sing, too," I said, figuring that singing praise and worship songs in church counted.

"I was thinking of showing the lads how we play cricket," Cliff said.

"That would be a good idea."

For the next half hour, the players and I gathered around Cliff Richard as he took a cricket bat and showed us some of the basics points to the game. I still had no idea that he was one of most famous pop figures in Europe.

Each of us got our turn, and it was fun to give cricket a try, but I could see why this game never caught on in the States.

As we were leaving, Cliff said to all of us, "Lads, who wants to see me in concert tomorrow night?"

The players and I looked at each other. We thought maybe he was talking about singing in a pub or for some local concert.

We nodded our approval, not to be impolite at the expression of generosity. So imagine our surprise the next evening when we had great seats for a massive show at Wembley Stadium in London with 100,000 other music fans. That's when we learned that Cliff Richard was a *huge* pop singer in Great Britain and throughout Europe. His heyday was in the late Fifties and early Sixties, when he dominated the British pop charts until a little band from Liverpool with John, Paul, George, and Ringo showed up on the scene.

The fellowship and the friendships the players and I made through our housing efforts provided some of our richest memories on the tour. I also knew that the players appreciated saving a boatload of French francs and English pounds because in those days, first-round and second-round prize money didn't go very far. The cost to rent a reasonable flat during "the fortnight" was too dear, as they say in England.

Wimbledon was where we did our biggest outreach of the year. We had our biggest attendance of players, coaches, and friends at our annual Pre-Wimbledon Dinner and Bible Study held on the Saturday night before the tournament began—usually two dozen men and women. One year, we had a lively discussion batting around this topic: "Does God ordain the draw at Wimbledon?" Our debate gave the players a sense that they were not alone out there. I used the analogy that many coals burn brightly together.

Wimbledon was and remains the only Grand Slam tournament that goes dark on the middle Sunday—no matches. That's a quaint holdover from Victorian times when Sundays were the Sabbath, a day of rest. At any rate, there were usually two outreaches on the middle Sunday. I can remember one year when Nduka Odizor, Kent Kinnear, and Gretchen Majors shared their faith in Christ at Queen's Road Baptist Church near the Wimbledon grounds. The main message was from longtime BBC broadcaster Gerald Williams.

The other outreach was held at All Souls Church in downtown London, which was broadcast to over 1 million people on BBC Radio. One year, Ken Flack and Michael Chang read Scriptures, and Stan Smith, Camille Benjamin, and Wendy White were interviewed by a BBC broadcaster about their faith.

One thing about being a tour chaplain is that I never knew how I would impact players' lives. There was one American player who had rabbit ears on the court. If one of the professional photographers courtside clicked his camera at the wrong time, this player would be bothered so much that he'd go into a funk and lose the next three games because he was thinking about how the photographer shouldn't have taken his picture just before he struck the ball.

I went to a local Christian bookstore and bought him a copy of *Three Steps Forward, Two Steps Back* by pastor Charles

I watched more than 21,000 matches during my twelve years on the tennis tour. My support meant a lot to the players and gave us something to talk about afterwards.

Every year, we gathered at Mark and Iona Birchall's house for fun and fellowship before Wimbledon. The players always said that was one of the highlights of the year. From the left, clockwise: Gretchen Magers, Kent Kinnear, Bridget and Kenny Thorne, Dan Pitts, myself, Bryan Shelton, and Brian Page.

Opening God's Word was a vital part of our ministry to the men's and women's tour. I sought to make our studies practical, interesting, relevant, and interactive.

Here I am being interviewed at the All Soul's Church
outreach event prior to the start of Wimbledon.

Swindoll. The book offered practical ways to walk with God through times of fear, stress, temptation, and yes, frustration and anger — like photographers making a racket on the court.

The player liked the book, and we had some good discussions. A few weeks later, I was watching him play a match when a courtside photographer bugged him again.

The player looked my way, clearly ticked by the distraction.

Oh, no, I thought. *Here go three games. Maybe the match.*

I reached down into my bag and waved a copy of Chuck Swindoll's book in his direction. The player saw it. His face lit up, as if to say, *I get it.*

He immediately regained his focus and didn't lose three games in a row — or the match. The way he carried himself was like, *Okay, Fritz, three steps forward.*

Be Ready for Anything

There were no days off when I was out on the road.

The weeks passed quickly due to watching matches and sharing as many meals as I could with the players. Usually one of the players supplied me with a "Coach's pass" that allowed me unlimited access to the locker room and the player's restaurant and lounges — areas excluded from the public. I never asked for a badge, as per Eddie's instructions, but the Christian players on tour wanted me to have one because they recognized that the players' lounge was where I did my most effective work.

One time, I passed through the players' food line at Queens Club, the grass-court warm-up tournament before Wimbledon.

"What's your fancy, guv'nor?" asked the sprightly lass as I pushed my tray along the cafeteria-like line.

I looked over the prepared sandwiches, but didn't see the one I wanted. "I'd like a ham and cheese sandwich," I said.

She scrunched her nose. "We don't put ham and cheese together in a sandwich. That's not cricket."

"Do you have a cheese sandwich?" I asked.

She handed me a cheese sandwich wrapped in plastic.

"Do you have a ham sandwich?" I asked.

"Yes, we do." She handed me a ham sandwich.

So I went to my table and put the two sandwiches together so that I got my ham and cheese sandwich.

Flexibility was the name of the game when you were on the road forty weeks a year, and the professional tennis tour can be likened to a traveling circus, staying in one city or resort area for a week (two weeks for the Grand Slams) before the troupe packs up for the next stop. It wasn't until the mid-1990s that the men's tour and women's tour agreed to hold several tournaments concurrently on the same site. The BNP Paribas Open in Indian Wells, California, and the Sony Ericsson Open in Key Biscayne, Florida, are a pair of present-day examples.

At the men's tournaments, I posted a note on the player's bulletin board in the locker room that I would be hosting a Bible study on Sunday night and Wednesday night. Sunday was often the day that most players arrived since the first round was played on Monday and Tuesday. You didn't want to do a second Bible study any later than Wednesday because the field could be cut by more than half the players after Wednesday.

Bible studies were usually held in a conference room at the player's hotel, or, on weeks when I knew there was just a handful of Christian players in the draw, we'd meet in a player's hotel room. I kept the Bible studies to no more than an hour or an hour-and-a-half long and used an interactive style to keep the players engaged.

Getting players to show up at a Bible study was like pulling hen's teeth because it was entirely up to them if they wanted to come or not. I knew that tennis was an individual sport—that was obvious. Everyone knew that. A chaplain for a baseball or football team has different dynamics because all the players are on the same team and thus pulling for each other—not playing against each other for their livelihood. Even in golf, which is an individual game, the players are playing against the course. In the game of tennis, though, your next-round opponent may be sitting in the chair next to you, and that creates an interesting situation. There's no way a tennis player wants to look vulnerable in front of his peers.

I often started out by announcing that we would be studying several passages from a book of the Bible, such as 1 Timothy. Many brought their Bibles with them, but I also provided Bibles for those who didn't have one.

As I talked, I kept up a steady patter. "Who wrote the book of Timothy?" I'd ask.

I didn't take any Bible knowledge for granted with the players. My goal was to get them to think.

I'd receive a couple of blank stares, but usually one of the players had the right answer: the apostle Paul.

"Paul was writing to Timothy. Who was he?" I'd ask.

Then I'd explain that Timothy became a believer after Paul's first missionary journey and joined him for his other two journeys as his assistant. Timothy knew Paul better than any other person, becoming like a son to him.

Then we'd go through several specific verses in Timothy, like in 1 Timothy 4:7-8 where Paul stresses the importance of spending your time and energy in the exercise of keeping spiritually fit. When Paul says that bodily exercise is all right but spiritual exercise is much more important and is a tonic for all you do, I'd see heads nod in recognition.

My goal in the Bible studies was to teach the players how to study the Bible so that when they were on their own, they had the tools to read God's Word and apply it to their lives.

I also counseled them to choose a life verse every chance I got. Some good choices were:

• "'I know the plans I have for you,' declares the Lord. 'Plans to prosper you and not to hurt you, to give you a future and a hope'" (Jeremiah 29:11).

• "Trust in the Lord with all your heart. Do not lean on your own understanding. In all your ways acknowledge Him, and he will direct your path" (Proverbs 3:5-6).

• "Delight yourself in the Lord and He give you the desires of your heart" (Psalm 37:4).

Then I would tell them that my life verse was from 1 Corinthians 15:10:

But by the grace of God I am what I am, and his grace to me was not without effect. No, I worked harder than all of them — yet not I, but the grace of God that was with me.

Some of the players told me that they got their life verses right away. "It's good to have a life verse that you can look at and know it's yours," I said.

At the Grand Slam tournaments, our Bible studies were co-ed because the women players could join us. Of course, I tailored my teaching in those situations and often talked about what the Bible says about relationships, marriage, money, and competition.

It was always tricky when I closed our time together by

asking if there were any prayer requests. Sure, a player might ask that we pray for someone else, like a parent facing a serious health challenge or a sister with a boyfriend issue, but the players rarely asked for prayer for themselves. They could not make themselves vulnerable in front of players that may be standing across the net from them the following week.

That's why we never heard a prayer request like *I've got this hamstring strain that's been bothering me* or *I need prayer for my down-the-line-backhand*. There was no way a player would voice those types of prayer requests in public. Otherwise, the other players in the room would take note or word would leak out.

Rain Delays and Meetings

One of the biggest things you learn on the tennis tour is how to kill time. Unless they are the first match of the day on a certain court, players aren't sure when they'll go on. They might be told that they are "third match on Court 2," meaning that two matches have to be completed before they're up. If the first match starts at 11 a.m., they could be waiting three hours or six hours before they get on.

I wouldn't engage players prior to a match unless they specifically *wanted* to talk to me. Some did. They liked talking about spiritual matters, either because they were generally interested in something more important than a tennis match, or they liked taking their mind off the task at hand. Some players found talking about God put them in the right frame of mind.

Players also seemed to be more open to talking to me during rain delays. There were more than a few Wimbledons where it rained for days at a time, and the players were

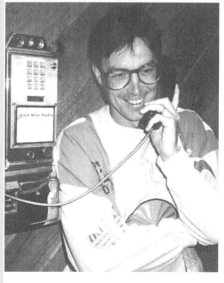

Staying in touch with the players and their families, arranging accomodations for the players at the different venues, and general scheduling meant being on the phone for quite a while.

cooped up in the players' lounge, hanging out and playing cards to kill the time.

But most of my "serious" meetings took place on their off days or after they played, or after they were out of the tournament. I'd try to find a spot where we could have some privacy, or I might meet the player at a restaurant in the city. My conversation would be unique to each person with the intention of moving them one step further along in their spiritual journey, closer to knowing Christ.

I always took every opportunity to share the love of Jesus Christ in a fashion that would meet each player where he was at. Keep in mind that I never knew if I would get another chance to speak into the player's heart. I also kept a handful of books on hand that could answer their questions and assist them in their journey to faith.

And that's where I usually left things, unless the player engaged me further. The last thing I wanted to do was push my beliefs on anybody. Ask anyone who was on the men's tour in the 1980s, and they'll tell you I was out there to be a friend to them.

A Tough Adversary

There was one opponent that the players couldn't beat—the women who hung out in packs at tournaments and hotel lobbies, hoping to catch the attention of the tennis players, who were often handsome young men in the prime of their youth. The pretty young women didn't have to work too hard to get the attention of the players, who were often famous and always available.

Certainly nothing was holding them back. The players were on their own, and even if they did have an entourage, they ran the show. Consequently, there was no one setting a curfew or no one running interference with the tennis groupies looking to hook up with the players, even if it was just for the night.

Few could resist their advances. In their defense, professional tennis players face challenges and temptations that the rest of us couldn't even begin to understand. They have money, tons of free time on their hands, and a lot of beautiful women to choose from. The ladies flirted like schoolgirls on holiday.

I remember one time when Juan Rios, a player from Puerto Rico, became a Christian through fellow players Bryan Shelton and Kenny Thorne. I met with Juan and told him how happy I was that he joined the family of God. Then Juan happened to mention that he was going to play a couple of tournaments in Europe.

"Be careful," I said. "You'll be tempted."

"No, I'll be okay," he replied.

I smiled, then I explained to Juan that since he had become a Christian, Satan was sure to test his newfound commitment.

Three weeks later, Juan sought me out. "Fritz, I couldn't believe it. Everything you said was true! I had girls coming at me from all directions!"

Juan was proud that he didn't yield to those temptations, but he was one of the few exceptions, I'm afraid. I don't know how many virgins were on the men's tour, but there weren't many.

Apart from the casual hook-ups, many of the players chose to travel the circuit with girlfriends to ease the loneliness of looking at the same four walls of their hotel room every night. I remember the time when one of the players who regularly attended our Bible studies brought his girlfriend out on tour with him. I wasn't stupid; I knew what was going on.

Then one evening, I received a message that this player wanted to see me at his hotel room. The girlfriend wasn't there, but the player told me that he wanted to bring her on a trip to the Far East.

"Do you like her?" I asked.

The player shrugged his shoulders. He knew how I felt about the situation, so he felt compelled to explain the situation. "Look, we could sleep in the same bed together and nothing would happen."

I arched an eyebrow. "You really believe that?"

He didn't respond.

"I think you're playing me," I said.

The room temperature got a lot colder.

"Our time is done, Fritz. I don't want to see you again."

If any of the players got to know me well, they understood real quickly where I stood about sleeping together before marriage. There was a player who came around to our Bible studies and knew about my stance on premarital sex. He traveled the circuit with his girlfriend, and I could tell the guilt was eating into him. I also knew they were staying in the same hotel room, so I knew they were sleeping together. I wasn't born in a barn, as my father would say.

One time at a tournament in Florida, for my weekly Bible study, I felt led to discuss the importance of staying pure before getting married. At seven o'clock, no one had showed up. Fifteen minutes later, this player and his girlfriend showed up—the first time in six months they'd come to one of my Bible studies.

I don't think they knew what my topic was that evening, but I wasn't about to change the subject. That night, we had an amazing heart-to-heart discussion. I told them about God's plan for waiting until marriage to share intimacy, and for those who'd had jumped the gun, we can repent of our actions with the confidence that God will forgive and forget our sins. I pointed to Psalm 103:11-12 (NIV), which says "For as high as the heavens are above the earth, so great is his love for those who fear him; as far as the east is from the west, so far has he removed our transgressions from us."

That couple repented and stayed pure until their marriage, and I'll never forget the sight of the bride walking down the aisle on the arm of her father, dressed in a white wedding gown. Her beaming smile told me that she knew she had been forgiven and that she was pure in God's eyes.

That couple was an exception, though. I'm afraid that the easy availability of women sent many players down a path "like an ox to the slaughter, like a deer stepping into a noose," as the wisest man who ever lived, King Solomon, said in Proverbs. That's why I prayed for those who were trying to stay strong as well as for those who knew or have heard the Truth but were living prodigal lives at the moment.

When you minister in the name of Christ, you can easily let yourself become disappointed in people when they slip or fall, but it's important to remember that we're all human. We all make mistakes and do things we regret in life. Sometimes, however, you can really get walloped upside the head and wonder, *How in the world did that happen?*

On one occasion, I got word that several players who'd attended my weekly Bible studies had been competing in a satellite Challenger Series event in Lagos, Nigeria, when something really strange happened. It seems that local authorities had found them naked in their hotel room, where they had torn-up their money, passports, traveler's checks, and a Bible and tossed everything out of their seventh-floor window. They had apparently been up for days without sleep and had gone crazy. One of them thought he was Jesus Christ and wanted to find his followers.

A U.S. embassy official called to the scene said he had heard these players had fallen under the influence of a radical Nigerian preacher, but as far as I knew, that was never confirmed. Since the players had destroyed their U.S. passports, they were quickly sent home to the States.

I learned about this incident from a *New York Times* reporter who called me for a comment. Initially, I was on the defensive because I wasn't there and didn't know the details, but I was also surprised to hear what happened. What the players had done was not encouraged by Scripture.

Eventually, I was able to speak with the players on the phone, and they sheepishly confirmed the details reported in the newspaper. I quickly realized there was no reasonable explanation for their behavior, so I focused my attention on helping them and their families, who were naturally upset.

Bizarre episodes like this reminded me that it wasn't easy being a tour chaplain. I was constantly engaging individuals in an individual sport dominated by outsized egos. I had to gauge my relationship with each person and calibrate what I said and how I said things because I wanted an ongoing opportunity to interact with them.

I was part of a small universe of people, each with different backgrounds or situations, and I had to be sensitive in my words, my actions, and my confidentiality. I wanted to maintain my integrity, continue to speak into these players' lives with the message of God's grace and love, and never burn any bridges.

The greatest part of being a tennis chaplain was the relationships I made with the players. I'm going to introduce several of them to you in the coming pages of *Love Game*.

Ready to get started? Good, because I just heard the umpire announce that our warm-up session is over.

One of the great tennis players of all time,
my friend, Stan Smith.

3
STAN SMITH
One of the Good Guys in Tennis

Iwouldn't have become a tennis chaplain or be writing this book without knowing Stan Smith, perhaps my greatest friend in Christian ministry. For nearly fifty years, he's been one of the good guys in the game of tennis, a man of his word because he's been in God's Word for nearly as long.

Stan grew up in Pasadena, California, a sun-splashed suburb of Los Angeles that's famous every New Year's Day for staging the Rose Parade and the "granddaddy of them all"—the Rose Bowl football game. Born in 1946 as the youngest of three boys, he was part of the post-war baby boom that would transform this country.

Tennis wasn't popular when Stan picked up a racket in his early teens. Baseball, basketball, and football ruled the sporting roost in the 1950s and early 1960s, so Stan, lanky for his age, played baseball as well as basketball growing up. But he wasn't the most nimble athlete early in his adolescence, having been rejected as a ball boy for a Davis Cup match because he was too clumsy.

A *Sports Illustrated* article called him a "big awkward donkey as a teenager, the sort of oaf who could not get out of the way of his sneakers," but that was an exaggeration. He was simply growing into his body, which would rise to six feet, four inches — tall for his time. Stan was blessed with excellent hand-eye coordination and had a big serve early on. He loved the one-on-one aspect of the game, of being the sole person responsible for winning or losing.

Perry Jones, the man who ruled Southern California tennis and kept an eye out for promising juniors in the pipeline, liked what he saw in Stan. Mr. Jones pulled him into his office at the Los Angeles Tennis Club and said he could make him into a champion if he would quit playing on the Pasadena High basketball team and concentrate on tennis. This happened six weeks into the basketball season.

Stan gulped. He loved playing on the varsity team and the camaraderie of the game, but he knew that his athletic future was in tennis. In tears, he called his high school basketball coach and told him that he was quitting the team midway through the season.

He began practicing at the Los Angeles Tennis Club every afternoon after school for two to four hours and taking lessons from legendary pro George Toley, who happened to moonlight as the coach of the University of Southern California tennis team. Toley, who knew firsthand about Stan's work ethic and potential to go far in the game, drew up plans to take his game to the next level.

Stan responded well to Toley's tutelage and then served notice that he was going places when he captured the U.S. Juniors (18 and under) championship at Kalamazoo, Michigan, the following summer.

Coach Toley didn't have to recruit Stan very hard to play for his USC team. He continued to revamp Stan's game, including changing his forehand midway through this fresh-man year by learning to "brush up" on the ball and impart more topspin. This was actually a major change in the way Stan hit the ball, but he diligently practiced his new forehand stroke for hours upon hours.

College tennis was where you honed your game back in those days, but Stan wasn't thinking about playing professional tennis when he enrolled at USC in the fall of 1964. Professionals were barred from playing the four Grand Slam tournaments, but nobody knew that in four short years the U.S. National Championships at Forest Hills would become known as the "U.S. Open" in 1968.

Stan was hoping to get good enough to represent his country in the Davis Cup and play on the *terre batue* of Roland Garros and the lawns of Wimbledon some day. He'd devote a few years to top-flight tennis competition on the amateur circuit and then become some sort of businessman, marrying and settling down in a white picket fence suburb like Pasadena.

Two things happened at USC that would change the arc of his life. The first was becoming a Christian during his sophomore year. A buddy asked him if he wanted to attend a Bible study for athletes led by Don Williams, the youth pastor at Hollywood Presbyterian Church. After hearing him present the Gospel, Stan realized that he was putting all his eggs into the tennis basket. For example, what would he do if he couldn't play tennis after being struck by a car and being paralyzed?

"And that's when I realized there is more to life than playing tennis," he told me. "I read a book of testimonies from different athletes, which drew me closer to God. That's when I committed my life to Christ."

I loved working with the kids at Young Life's Oakbridge tennis camp with Stan Smith.

We called ourselves the "Oakbridge Boys" when we helped Stan at the Young Life tennis camp.

 **'85年度**

윔블던참피온 스탠·스미스招請 韓·美親善테니스大會

KOREAN-AMERICAN
Good-Will Tennis Game Featuring Wimbledon Champion STAN SMITH

日時 : 1985年 11月 9日 (土)
　　　 13 : 00時
場所 : 奬忠테니스코트
主催 : 한국스포츠선교회
　　　 日 刊 스 포 츠
主管 : 大韓테니스協會
後援 : 韓一테니스볼
　　　 한국도자기 (주)
　　　 明 知 建 設 (株)
　　　 髙 麗 合 纖 (株)
　　　 월 드 테 니 스

During a mission trip to South Korea, Stan Smith told us that
our purpose was to use our abilities and talents to
communicate what Jesus Christ had done for us.

The other thing that Stan did while he was at USC was set four goals that he wanted to accomplish with tennis:

1. Become a member of the United States Davis Cup team.
2. Become the No. 1 player in the United States.
3. Win Wimbledon
4. Become the No. 1 player in the world.

He would put a check mark next to each goal—and discover something about himself and the meaning of life.

The Game Goes Open

Talk about good timing.

In the spring of 1968, Stan was in the right place at the right time. The Grand Slam tournaments had recently agreed to allow professional players to compete with amateurs, which heralded the start of the Open Era. Stan turned pro a few weeks after capturing the 1968 NCCA singles championship and doubles championship with teammate Bob Lutz.

The sporting public was fascinated that professionals and amateurs could play on the same court, but it didn't take long for the professionals to stake their claim that they played the best tennis in the world. Stan, with his classic serve-and-volley game, quickly established himself as a force in singles and doubles. He won his first of five Grand Slam doubles titles in the inaugural 1968 U.S. Open with longtime partner Bob Lutz at his side.

Smith and Lutz defeated Arthur Ashe and Andrés Gimeno of Spain in the 1968 final, 11-9, 6-1, 7-5. Ashe—an African-American who played at UCLA when Stan was at cross-town rival USC—won the first U.S. Open that year as an amateur. This meant Arthur was ineligible to receive the winner's prize money of $14,000 in the $100,000 event, at the time the richest tournament in tennis history. (As a way of contrast, the 2012 winner will take home $1.8 million.)

Stan and Arthur were the young faces of tennis in the U.S. at the start of the 1970s, starring on Davis Cup teams and taking their places in the world's Top Ten. The tennis boom was right around the corner, and Stan's best years were coming up. His breakthrough season came in 1971 when he reached the Wimbledon final but fell in five sets to Australia's mustachioed John Newcombe. Two months later, he captured his first Grand Slam title, winning the U.S. Open over Jan Kodes of Czechoslovakia.

The year 1972 is when everything came together. Stan outdueled the mercurial Ilie Nastase of Romania in the Wimbledon singles final, 4-6, 6-3, 6-3, 4-6, 7-5, and lifted the silver loving cup of the world's most prestigious tournament above his shoulders. He was now the world's reigning No. 1 player who even had a tennis shoe named after him—the Adidas Stan Smith. The white leather tennis shoe with a green tab on the heel is still around four decades later, having reached iconic status for retro tennis shoe fans. I've worn more than a few pairs of the 40 million pairs that have been sold since 1972.

Stan was never the type who wore his faith on the sleeve of a Fred Perry white polo shirt, but word seeped out that being a Christian was important to him. If you go back and read feature stories written about Stan from that time period, he was described as "deeply religious," "God-fearing," "temperate and disciplined," a "respectful, loving son," and a "self-made champion" whose "corny dream" was to one day manage his own YMCA.

Stan's sublime qualities were put to their ultimate test in the 1972 Davis Cup final following the U.S. Open that year. It's hard to describe what a big deal this was at the time, but let me tell you, this was huge for two reasons:

1. The United States team would be playing behind the Iron Curtain in Bucharest, Romania, the first time in thirty-five years that a Davis Cup final had been held anywhere except in the U.S. and Australia.

2. There were two Jewish players on the team—Harold Solomon and Brian Gottfried, which created security concerns. A month earlier, eight Arab commandos had broken into the Olympic Village in the midst of the Olympic Games in Munich, West Germany, shooting and killing two Israelis outright and holding nine members of the Israeli Olympic team hostage. They would all be killed in a firefight at the airport.

The Davis Cup tie would be the biggest sporting event ever staged on Romanian soil. With the eyes of the world focused on Bucharest, President Nicolae Ceausescu, a hard-line Communist, would brook no "incidents." He ordered his secret police to escort the U.S. contingent everywhere. If anything happened to the American team, Ceausescu said, heads would roll—and no one doubted that he meant it literally. Security was tighter than a gut string job.

Romania had never won a Davis Cup in the history of the nation-against-nation competition. Here was a golden chance with Ilie Nastase and Ion Tiriac on their side. Nastase was ranked No. 2 in the world, right behind Stan, and as for Tiriac, one could write a book about this colorful character with a mean streak. Tiriac was from Transylvania, the home of Count Dracula, and he looked like a villain out of a horror movie with bushy black curls and a dark, swarthy moustache that wrapped around his jowls like a black centipede. Armed with a weird scoop-shovel forehand and chip back-hand, Tiriac didn't bring much game to the court, but he could drive you crazy if you let him.

The aging tennis stadium was filled with boisterous and patriotic Romanians, and the linesmen chairs were filled with patriotic Romanians who felt obliged to make the "right call" for the home team. The atmosphere was electric for the first rubber between Stan and Ilie Nastase. This was a major test of the two best players in the world on a huge stage. The Davis Cup was at stake.

Stan knew that playing against Nastase on a slow red clay court would blunt the speed of his serve and take away his ability to charge the net. Knowing what he had to do, Stan played splendid tennis in the opening match, shattering the Romanian's fragile psyche by playing error-free tennis. The pressure to win for the home country proved to be too much for Ilie, and Stan left the court with a straight-set victory to put the United States ahead, 1-0.

Next up was Tom Gorman versus Ion Tiriac—a must-win match for the Romanians. As the match progressed, the line calls started becoming more and more ridiculous. It was obvious to Stan that his teammate was getting cheated. After all, the ball leaves a large imprint every time it strikes the red clay, yet anytime Gorman hit a ball near the line, a Romanian line judge yelled "Out!" There was no Hawk-Eye challenge system in those days.

Conversely, the court was six inches longer and wider for Tiriac. Since players are trained from a young age to "hit for the lines," Gorman was reduced to fighting a lion of a player without a chair and a whip.

The match slipped out of Gorman's grasp as spectators coughed and cleared their throats in unison as the American was making his service toss. Those distractions and a bunch of bad calls on big points unraveled Gorman's game. The

American lost in five sets after winning the first two, and everyone knew this match had been stolen.

After the U.S. split the opening day matches, it was up to Stan and partner Erik Van Dillen to win the all-important doubles point. They played the match of their lives, defeating Nastase and Tiriac in three straight sets. Now the U.S. needed to win only one more rubber to bring home the Davis Cup, but both sides knew the winner of the Stan Smith-Ion Tiriac match would decide the tie. Ilie Nastase would not lose to Tom Gorman.

The night before Stan's match with Tiriac, the Davis Cup referee, Enrique Morea of Argentina, pulled Stan over the side at the player's hotel. He had a message to deliver.

"Tomorrow, you have to win easily," said the referee.

"What do you mean, win easily?" Stan replied. He expected Tiriac to pull every gamesmanship trick in the book, including getting the linesmen to make outrageous calls on whether the ball was in or out, depending on who hit it.

"Because I'm not going to change any calls," said Morea.

Stan placed his hands on his hips. "If you're not going to change any calls, then who is?"

With that, Morea shrugged his shoulders.

Stan played like he knew that any shots close to the line wouldn't be called his way. Of course, that made his task more difficult since the court was one size on his side of the net and far smaller on the other side. He took other precautions, like serving a good six inches or even a foot behind the baseline so that he couldn't be called for a foot fault. All Stan could do was serve hard and hope for the best.

They split the first two sets and came to a crucial juncture in the third set. Tiriac was serving at 4-5, 30-40, set point for

Stan. Tiriac hit a first serve that was a little long. Stan, knowing that he had to play everything, knocked a backhand up the line for a clean winner. Obviously, both the linesman and Tiriac were hoping that Stan would hit the out serve into the net or long so that they could claim the point, but when Stan hit the winner, that ruined their plans. Tiriac stormed the net and demanded that the linesman call the out serve out, and the linesman complied. It had to be the latest "out" call in history.

On the second serve, however, Tiriac dumped the ball halfway up the net. There was no way a linesman could change that result. Third set to the United States.

The fourth set was all Tiriac. At one point, Ion hit a drop shot. Stan ran for his life, but he didn't reach the ball before it bounced twice. In frustration, he slammed the ball into the net. Tiriac then began arguing with the referee that Stan was trying to hit him, which riled up the crowd to a fever pitch. Tiriac began stalling. When the umpire motioned for him to play, Tiriac said, "Go ahead and default me. Then see what happens!" The referee Enrique Morea begged Tiriac to return to the court.

The stage was set for a climatic fifth set. Stan served the first game, but quickly dug himself into a big hole—down 15-40. Both sides knew that if Tiriac got a break, he and the Romanian crowd would not be denied.

To this day, Stan can't remember what happened. But the record shows that Stan served himself out of the jam and rode the momentum to a 6-0 final set triumph, losing only eight points and clinching the Davis Cup tie for the United States.

As he walked to the net after the final point, he wondered if he should shake hands with Tiriac. Stan decided to, but he had a message for his foe. "I don't respect you as a person anymore," said Stan, turning his back and walking away.

His Davis Cup coach, Dennis Ralston, believes that the epic match in Bucharest was a battle of good triumphing over evil. Stan doesn't quite see it in those terms; he was busy playing the match, not watching it.

"Honestly, I know that Stan is the only guy who could have won that match," Ralston said. "I don't even think that Rod Laver could have remained as calm or stayed as focused as Stan did that afternoon. What kept Stan going was his deep reservoir of faith."

Stan was always part of the All Soul's Church outreach event that took place in London before the start of Wimbledon. Cami Benjamin and Wendy White look on.

A Little Perspective

When the triumphant U.S. Davis Cup team returned home from Romania in 1972, Stan was on top of the tennis world. All four goals had been met: he had played Davis Cup for his country; was the No. 1 player in the United States; won Wimbledon; was ranked as the No. 1 player in the world. He had also captured his one and only U.S. Open a month before, which solidified his stronghold as the world's best player.

He had reached the mountaintop. What did the view look like?

"You know the old song that says *Is That All There Is?* by Peggy Lee?" Stan said. "I thought about that song after I had reached all four of my goals. I had an interesting revelation at the time. I realized that my faith and my family were a lot more important than winning tournaments. I was so thankful that I knew Christ."

There's one more story about Stan that many have not heard, but it says a lot about the size of his heart. In 1977, a few years before I joined the tour, Stan was playing a tournament in South Africa. Remember, this was the height of the apartheid years when blacks were suppressed and whites had priority for housing, jobs, and education as well as political power.

Stan was hitting some balls with Bob Lutz on the practice court when he noticed a young black man leaning against the fence—a young man eager to play tennis. Thinking that he'd encourage the youngster, Stan asked him if he wanted to hit a few balls with them.

The youth jumped at the chance. It turned out that he was a junior player in the tournament, having been given a wild card by the organizers. He said his name was Mark

Even at major events like Wimbledon, Stan always had time to chat with me and check in on how things were going with the tennis ministry.

Mathabane.

"He wasn't a very good player, but he was eager to play," Stan told me. "When we were done, I asked him to join me in the player's lounge. I didn't realize it at the time, but Mark was not allowed in the player's lounge even though he was in the tournament. People were staring at us. We started talking, and he brought up the subject of education. He wanted to play tennis in college in the United States. Could I help him?"

Stan could see the desperation in the young man's eyes. Winning a tennis scholarship to a U.S. college was his only ticket out of South Africa.

Stan offered to help. Upon his return to the States, he talked to his old tennis coach at USC, George Toley, who wrote ten colleges around the country on Mark's behalf. Limestone College in South Carolina offered Mark a full scholarship, which changed his life forever.

Stan's involvement didn't end there. He and his wife, Marjory, continued to provide financial as well as emotional support upon Mark's arrival in the United States. "He had problems with the whole transition to life in America," Stan said. "But he was quite a writer. I had read the letter that he sent to the tennis coach at Limestone College and thought somebody had written it for him because the English was so good. Turns out that English was his second language because he had read a lot of books in English growing up. His passion was writing."

Fast forward to 1986, when Mark Mathabane wrote an

Stan came down to Florida to be part of a
"Breakfast of Champions" before my wedding.

autobiography called *Kaffir Boy: The True Story of a Black Youth's Coming of Age in Apartheid South Africa.* His story focused on the brutality of the apartheid regime and how he escaped by embracing education to lift himself from a desperate situation in apartheid South Africa.

The book became a national best seller here in the United States. An up-and-coming talk show host named Oprah Winfrey read the book and invited him on her show. President Bill Clinton read *Kaffir Boy* and invited Mark to serve as a White House Fellow during his first term to advise him on educational policies.

Today, Mark is a much-in-demand speaker and married to Gail, a writer he met in New York City. They are the parents of three children, including their youngest son Stanley — named after the American tennis player who changed Mark's life.

I would say that's pretty cool.

Stan and Marjory Smith married in 1974 and have four children: Ramsey (named after the first tour chaplain, Ramsey Earnhardt), who is the men's tennis coach at Duke University; Trevor, who is working in New York with a private equity company and is married with two children; Logan, who married in 2011 and lives in Savannah, Georgia; and Austin, who works in New York City for Golf Digest *magazine in sales and support.*

Stan remains involved with tennis, directing the Smith Stearns Tennis Academy near their home in Hilton Head Island, South Carolina. He is also the president of Stan Smith Events, which help corporations entertain their clients at major sporting events like tennis' Grand Slam tournaments, the Olympic Games, FIFA World Cup matches, and major golf tournaments.

Stan was recently elected president of the International Tennis

Hall of Fame in Newport, Rhode Island, and he can often be seen sitting in the Royal Box at Wimbledon during the women and men's final singles matches.

For more information, check out stansmithevents.com.

Hank Pfister had one of the sweetest one-handed backhands on the tour.

4
HANK PFISTER
The Tennis Player Who Tampered His Temper

When you think of Wimbledon, you think of green grass, white lines, and strawberries and cream. The fortnight of tennis at the All England Lawn Tennis Club is when the sport takes on a high church ambience. The players are dressed in their Sunday best: all attire must be predominantly white with no fluorescent colors. Shorts and skirts must be totally white.

The players are expected to be on their best behavior while playing in this "cathedral of tennis." They are also expected to show a proper reverence for Wimbledon's 130-year-old traditions of fair play and stoicism on the court. Stiff upper lip and all that.

Wimbledon's greatest tradition is playing on a grass surface, which is an anachronism in this modern age. When I was playing tennis at Malone College, three of the four Grand Slams were played on grass; today, Wimbledon is the last custodian of grass court tennis and one of a handful of grass court tournaments still on the calendar.

So imagine the time when I was watching American player

Hank Pfister play a match on one of the outer courts shortly after I started following the tour.

Hank was a hardworking, blue collar pro from Bakersfield, California, who never had anything handed to him in life. He didn't play with a lot of flash although he was a stylish player who knifed his volleys. What he did was work harder than you. More often than not, he beat you into submission with an aggressive serve-and-volley game.

Oh, and he had a volcanic temper.

I'm not talking about a bad display of manners that you might see in a John McEnroe match. Hank never got into an umpire's face with a "You cannot be serious—that ball was on the line" soliloquy. He'd blow his top after dumping a volley into the net or missing an up-the-line passing shot on a pivotal point.

The incident in which I saw Hank go ballistic happened in Wimbledon's Round of 16. (In fact, Hank played in the second week at Wimbledon four times, which shows you how talented he was.) He had gotten a bad bounce—one of many that day—that cost him a break of service, so Hank took out his frustrations on the court. He beat the grass with his racket like a father who loses control and whips his son with a belt.

Thwack!

Thwack!

Thwack!

And another *thwack* for good measure.

The crowd, aghast at the breach of decorum, turned silent. Tufts of grass had flown up as he inflicted deep wounds on the court surface. I'm sure the Wimbledon groundskeepers gave him a black mark and put him on their watch list.

"I was a hothead and acted like an idiot back then," Hank said. "What can I say?"

But Hank changed his explosive ways, and I was able to witness how Jesus Christ can change a player's life and demeanor in a dramatic fashion.

Growing Up in Bakersfield

Hank Pfister started swinging a badminton racket when he was three years old. He was introduced to the game by his father, a teaching pro who was good enough to play on the pro tour back in the day—but there wasn't much pro tennis in the wartime 1940s and sunny 1950s. Sure, a half-dozen of the top professional players like Jack Kramer and Pancho Gonzalez barnstormed during that era, but for all intents and purposes, there was no organized professional tennis as we know it today.

Hank played a lot of junior tennis tournaments in Southern California, a hotbed of tennis activity. When he got to his first big finals in the 12 and unders, he served and volleyed on both first and second serves—and promptly lost 6-0, 6-0. Another father approached Hank's dad and said if Hank stayed back and hit some groundstrokes, he might win some tournaments some day.

"I'm going to leave him be," his father replied. "He'll figure it out."

Hank didn't have the patience to grind out groundstrokes, so he kept to the serve-and-volley path laid out by this father. As he grew into his body (eventually sprouting to six feet, four inches), he became a very good player but one who was overlooked by those who ran junior tennis. Maybe that's because he didn't come from Beverly Hills or La Jolla, posh enclaves that produced a lot of top players. People make fun of Bakersfield, a hot, dusty city in California's Central Valley.

While Stanford, USC, and UCLA offered Hank a full ride scholarship, Hank passed them up and chose San Jose State because he wanted to play high on the ladder—which might not have happened at the Big Three California tennis powers.

It turned out to be a good decision. Hank played No. 1 at San Jose State, which meant that he played against the No. 1 players at Stanford, USC, and UCLA. During his junior year, he was undefeated against their top players, yet in the 1975 NCAA Championships, he was seeded No. 2 behind UCLA's Billy Martin, a player whom he had beaten in dual matches.

You can blame tennis politics.

Then on the morning of his NCAA quarterfinal match in Corpus Christi, Texas, the winds were blowing steady at 30 mph. Tournament officials told him to go play SMU's George Hardie, a player he would normally handle. But with strong winds hampering the ball toss and making a mockery of the game, Hank lost 7-6, 6-7, 7-6. All three sets were decided on the ninth point of the nine-point, sudden-death tiebreaker that was used in college tennis in those days. In other words, the third-set tiebreaker went to 4-4, meaning it was simultaneous match point for *both* players.

The mid-'70s were an exciting time for tennis as the pro game was gaining in popularity. Hank was beating players who were turning pro, so he naturally thought *Why not me?* But he blew out his ankle changing direction on the court just before the start of his senior season. He stopped so suddenly that he broke his ankle and ruptured the joint, tearing three tendons. Doctors said they had never seen such a horrific injury. Hank was confined to a wheelchair for a couple of months as he recovered from major surgery.

"Doctors gave me an 80 percent chance of having a normal ankle but said playing high-level tennis would be doubtful," Hank said. "I was very discouraged, as you can imagine."

Where was Hank's faith at the time?

"Nowhere! In college, I was thinking about girls and where the next party was and about my tennis," he said. "I didn't think very much about the Lord, so God was not in my life. What affected me most was when I went home and went to church with Mom. I knew I should be in the Lord, but it got easy to be out of the Lord and doing things in the world, out of His light. There was a battle going on in my heart. Sometimes I'd come home and tell myself that I have to start reading God's Word again, but then I'd get back in the dorms, and guys were having beers down the hall. I was just too weak at the time."

Hank put all his determination into rehabbing his ankle while losing his senior year of college tennis. He wanted to play in the NCAA Championships, even though his ankle wasn't fully healed. He played one team match to qualify for the season-ending tournament, but he lost in the first round of the NCAAs, limping around the court.

"After graduation, the one thing I had going for me was that I wasn't afraid of hard work," he said. "My medical people laid out a strict regimen to physically rehab my ankle."

This time, the ankle responded well, and he was soon playing and beating all his adversaries again. "I wasn't sure what I was going to do after college, but my dad and I thought I had the skills to turn pro," Hank said.

He caught a break when the USTA picked him for the Junior Davis Cup team, which was kind of a training ground for the top young players in the U.S. He played No. 1, ahead of contemporaries like Butch Walts, Victor Amaya, Bruce Manson, Elliot Teltscher, and Peter Fleming. That, and winning a few satellite tour events, gave him enough points to get into the main draw of the Grand Slams and other professional tournaments.

His first full year on the tour—the 1977 season—saw him break into the Top 50, and he was a solid player ranked in the mid-30s when I started as a tour chaplain in 1980. A year later, we met at a tournament in Cleveland when he approached me with a big study Bible and asked me where the Bible study was that night.

I tried to act unsurprised, but inside I thought, *Isn't this the guy who has a temper on the court*? But then he told me that his father, Hank, Sr., had died recently, and that got him thinking about God.

"What changed my life was that my father started having health problems in his early fifties," Hank said. "Let me give you some background on my dad: he never went to church, never read the Bible, and never wanted anything to do with God. Anything I learned about Christianity growing up came from my mother, Florence, taking me and my two sisters, Gay and Judy, to church.

"All that changed for him when he underwent serious heart surgery for blocked arteries. He had to face his mortality and make some major lifestyle changes because he smoked and drank, and when he drank, he was a pretty tough guy. But that changed when he started looking into the Word and became a Christian. He and I became closer at this point, and he knew I was struggling out there on the tour. Then he came down with lung cancer, and doctors told him that they had caught it too late. They tried chemotherapy, but it didn't work. His body was dying."

Toward the end, father and son shared several intimate conversations while Hank Sr. was on his deathbed. The father who had taught his son how to play the game had one more lesson he wanted to instill before he left this Earth.

"Hank, I know you're struggling with your faith, but you've got to give it up to the Lord," Hank Sr. said. "You're fighting yourself to make yourself a better man, but your mistake is that you need to give it up to the Lord so that you can become the man He wants you to be for your wife and your future family."

Hank had been married to Kim for several years, and she traveled the tour with him.

"Hearing my father say that about literally killed me," Hank said. "For the first time, I realized that I could not accomplish something I wanted to accomplish on my own."

But there was a battle still raging in his heart. The score was still *Advantage, the world.*

"I didn't see how I could go to a Bible study after being a jerk on the court, throwing temper tantrums, and cussing like a drunken sailor," Hank said. "My plan was to fix myself first."

But that wasn't working, which is why Hank sought me out in Cleveland.

Hank came to that player's Bible study, and then we met one-on-one several times. I can remember talking to Hank about how he could play tennis as a Christian. The first step was to understand what God did for him to give him the athletic talent and strong mind to play tennis at the professional level. "You want to play out of God's grace and thankfulness for His gifts," I said. "Sure, there are going to be times when you lose your temper, but God will understand. He understands how you are wired."

Hank said he always thought that being a Christian and an athlete would be the worst combination in the world. "I just didn't get it at the time," he said. "You figure out stuff as you go, and I finally came to a point where I had to give myself and my tennis to the Lord, just as my father said I should do. I had to thank God for the skills that He gave me, and that's when I surrendered."

Hank and I met regularly after that, and overnight, I witnessed a dramatic change in his on-the-court behavior.

"I chose to enjoy the battle on the court," Hank said. "I had always liked to fight and loved it when it got questionable as to whether I was going to win or lose. At first, I didn't know how to do that as a Christian, but eventually it became real to me."

I credit Hank for hanging in there because he said he lost "something like fifteen matches" in a row after dedicating himself to Christ at the age of twenty-seven. But his best years were yet to come as he reached a career-high No. 19 in 1983 at the age of twenty-nine.

But more importantly, he was part of the first wave of Christians on the tour, joining players like Stan Smith, Sandy and Gene Mayer, Mike Cahill, and Terry Moor. "We were a pretty tight group for a while," he said, "and surprisingly, becoming a Christian gave me the opportunity to play the best tennis I could."

Serving at 4-5, Hank was down double-match point at 15-40. Hank served and volleyed, as he always did, but Henri hit the return so low over the net *and* at Hank's feet that all the American could do was instinctively put his racket behind him and hit the ball between his legs. He half-volleyed into the open court but gave Henri enough time to run it down. Hank knew he had to guess which side to cover.

He lurched to his right just as the ball was whizzing past. He somehow nicked the ball with the tip of his racket—the expensive part, as ESPN commentator Brad Gilbert likes to say—for a winner.

Hank was thrilled to still be in the match, but both of us knew that he was still in deep trouble because Leconte had another match point in his pocket. But the Frenchman dropped to his knees like he had been shot in the chest.

Hank looked over and nodded as if to say, *I'm going to win this match.* He bombed in a few more serves, broke Leconte, and served out the match to notch a win against the 17th-ranked player in the world. "I saw him literally leave the court crying and then walk outside the court and hit his head lightly against a tree," Hank said.

The Invasion of the Tennis Clones

For more than twenty years, Hank has been the director of tennis at the Stockdale Country Club in Bakersfield, coaching juniors and giving tennis lessons.

In a way, Hank is carrying on his father's legacy. Hank Sr. started the tennis program at Stockdale Country Club and served as its first head pro with the premise that he would get the tennis program going and find a new pro to take his place. Hank Sr. was a full-time teacher and coach at Bakersfield Junior College and needed to get back to just doing that only.

Elsewhere on the family front, Kim gave birth to a trio of daughters during the 1980s: Andrea, Kelly, and Patty. Hank had a self-imposed rule as their children were growing up—his last lesson of the day ended at 6 p.m.

"I made sure I was home every night for dinner when the kids were growing up," he said. "I also had breakfast with them and spent a lot of time with my daughters. Kim and I took them to church since they were little kids and tried to live our lives in a Christian manner. If you're not backing it up, then it's pretty hard to sell the product. We know that our girls got it at an early age. They were great kids, going on missions trips. Their walks with God have always been very solid. As a parent, you want to pass on the good stuff and bury the bad stuff. That's what I tried to do. I did tell them what an idiot I was in the early parts of my adult life in the hope that they wouldn't have to go through those experiences. And fortunately my girls have not had to do that. I'm very proud of them. They all went to college, got their degrees, and married wonderful husbands."

As for his teaching career, Hank, who's fifty-eight, says his current beef is that all the players coming up are playing the same way—standing five feet behind the baseline and pounding big groundstrokes off both wings. "Everybody has theories about why this has occurred, but when I was growing up, we were driven to the local tennis courts or club and played lots of practice sets with lots of different players. You figured out how to play because we weren't told how to play. That's why you saw all sorts of different styles back in my day. You had Stan Smith, who could serve and volley as well as stay back, and then there was Harold Solomon, whose feet never touched the court inside the baseline.

"Today, it's a cloning system where they put everybody on the court and they just bang groundstrokes. Parents want to see their kids win early, just as the USTA does. The only way you win early is to hit groundstrokes. If a kid serves and volleys at age twelve like I did, he'll get beat oh-and-oh and be told never to try doing that again. Today they won't let kids hit slice backhands because they say the ball floats too much, yet if you hit the slice backhand right, it can be an effective shot."

Hank wrote about this in an article for *Tennis Week* called "The Invasion of the Tennis Clones."

"When a player like Pete Sampras or Roger Federer comes along, it highlights how much of the rest of the players are clones," he wrote. "While there are many arguments about why this cloning has occurred, it has to do with the pivotal role of society in general and parents and coaches specifically. Our society, which elevates athletes to superheroes, puts winning ahead of all else, equates success to income, and promotes a 'me-first' attitude, is leading parents and coaches in the wrong direction."

Hank then offered tennis parents some excellent advice. First was the idea that only a handful of players make it to the professional ranks—so the odds are miniscule. Second, there are only so many years of intense competition that athletes can endure both physically and mentally, so why push things from ages six to sixteen? The ages eighteen to twenty-eight are when young adults are at their physical peak and more mentally mature.

Finally, Hank had this advice to impart: "If everything you do with your child revolves around the sport being played and the importance of winning and losing, especially at early ages, you are missing the point of sports. The point of sports is to teach the 'process' of learning, which is to practice, prepare, compete, think on your own, adjust to mistakes, reapply new skills and knowledge at the next competitive opportunity, all of which leads to improvement."

Sounds like great advice for passing our faith to our children as well.

Hanging out with (from the left) Rhonda and Gene Mayer,
Hank Pfister, and myself at Gene's home in New York.

5
GENE MAYER
A Hunger for God

There's one place where Gene Mayer never lost a match—the restaurant table. Gene, who rose to No. 4 in the world in 1981, had a bottomless pit for a stomach, and he could out-eat anyone.

You'd never think that by looking at him. He was a skinny six feet tall and weighed a buck-fifty-five. He wasn't an imposing figure on the court. He had this curious walk between points that was something between Andre Agassi's waddle and Ivan Lendl's mini-swagger.

But he could move you around the court like you were on the end of a puppet string—and he was the maestro. Gripping the racket with two hands on his backhand *and* forehand, he created angles that you didn't think were possible within the confines of a singles court. Gene had an uncanny ability to make you feel like a fool when you played against him.

And then he'd eat you out of house and home if you let him.

I remember the time Gene asked me to watch his night

match at the old U.S. Pro Indoors tournament played inside Philadelphia's drafty Spectrum, a massive arena that accommodated more than 18,000 fans for 76ers games. The tournament was running behind, as indoor tournaments in the middle of winter often do, so Gene didn't get on the carpeted tennis court until midnight. By the time he served out the match at 1:30 in the morning, there couldn't have been more than a hundred spectators left in the cavernous arena.

"You want to go get something to eat?" he asked after the match.

It was late. I was tired. I wanted to get back to the player's hotel and get my sleep.

"Of course," I said. "What do you feel like?"

"Philly cheesesteak," he said.

For those of you who haven't been to the City of Brotherly Love, Philly cheesesteaks are a civic icon and a cultural obsession. A cheesesteak is a long, crusty roll filled with thinly sliced sautéed ribeye beef and melted cheese.

We found an all-night diner close to the player's hotel. I ordered one Philly cheesesteak — and let my jaw drop when Gene ordered six.

Then I watched him plow through a half-dozen of those monstrous sandwiches like he had entered the Coney Island hot-dog eating contest every Fourth of July. He wolfed them down in no time.

Gene could swallow up opponents in a similar fashion with the amazing spins he put on the ball. He imparted Rafa-like topspin with a snowshoe-sized Prince Graphite racket fabricated from 1970s technology, manufacturing incredible angles that frustrated opponents to no end. What made him even more maddening to play was that he was a touch player who played against the grain. His opponents complained they couldn't tell where he was going to hit the ball. He disguised his shots well and got his adversaries off their game.

He learned to put spin on the ball from his father, Alex, a teaching pro who immigrated to the United States in December 1951. "When I was a newborn, Dad hung a rubber ball over the crib so that I would get used to the movement of the ball. Then he gave me a small wooden paddle when I was two and let me hit that ball. When I turned three, I started hitting a tennis ball on the court with a sawed-off wooden racket."

Gene developed a strong appetite for the game while he and his big brother, Sandy, kept their mother, Inge, as busy as a Denny's short-order cook. For breakfast, they wolfed down a dozen scrambled eggs, a plate of pancakes, a loaf of bread, two quarts of milk, and a variety of ham and cheeses to fill their young bellies.

Thank goodness Gene and Sandy had fast-acting metabolisms that burned up the calories like a Pennsylvania coal furnace. They moved quickly through life. When the Mayer brothers weren't in school, they could be found on their backyard tennis court practicing and playing sets every day as long as the weather cooperated in their hometown of Woodmere, New York, located near JFK International Airport and around twenty-three miles from midtown Manhattan. During the cold winter months, they scrounged for indoor court time, often playing before school or at odd hours on the weekends.

Gene was a childhood prodigy on the tennis court. By the age of nine, he was the best player in the world in his age group. He won the 1965 Orange Bowl 10-and-unders, the unofficial world championships for juniors played in Miami during the Christmas break—and didn't lose a game the entire tournament, winning every match 6-0, 6-0. (That record will never be broken because there are no longer any international or national junior events for 10-and-unders.)

Gene followed Sandy to Stanford University, enrolling in the fall of 1973 as the top junior recruit in the country for a team that had won the 1973 NCAA Championships. Stanford coach Dick Gould had assembled another power-house team with his brother, Sandy, John Whitlinger, Pat Dupre, Chico Hagey, Jim Delaney, Nick Saviano, and Chip Fisher.

If Gene thought he was something special the moment he stepped on the Stanford campus, he was quickly disabused of that notion. "I came in as the best recruit in the country, but I had to fight for a spot in the top six," he recalled. "As for my studies, I came in with a 4.0 grade-point average in high school and scoring 1530 on my SATs, but on my first day at Stanford, I was talking with a couple of other incoming freshmen, and they casually let me know that they had scored perfect 1600s on their SATs. That was sobering to hear. I had lots of studying to do, and I was also missing my girlfriend, Rhonda, who's now my wife. Being away from her and my family put me under all sorts of pressure. It was an incredibly intense time for me."

Gene and Rhonda had started dating each other when they were fourteen years old and kept the relationship going even after Gene and his parents moved more than hour away to Wayne, New Jersey, when he was fifteen years old. (His father had accepted a new teaching position.) Gene and Rhonda saw each other on weekends and talked as often as they could in that pre-cell phone era.

When Gene flew off to Stanford, Rhonda was still in high school because Gene had graduated a year early after skipping a grade. Again, their relationship was tested since they had to write letters or talk on the phone whenever they could catch each other. "I missed her a great deal and wished I could be with her. A lot of people love their college days, but for me it was a lot of unhappy times," Gene said. "I saw myself as a student and as a tennis player, but when I arrived at Stanford, my self-identity was shaken."

Grappling with the major issues of life prompted him to seek out the chaplain of the Stanford tennis team, Jim Stump, who made himself available to the players. It was up to the student-athletes if they wanted to see Jim, an easygoing youth minister who made it known that if any of the players had questions about life or girlfriends or anything else on their minds, he was just the right person to talk to between classes or over lunch.

He told Jim that he had been raised a nominal Roman Catholic by parents who took him and Sandy to church early in their lives, but their attendance at Mass had fallen off dramatically during the teen years because of their lack of interest. He added that no one in the family ever talked about religion or what it meant to be a Christian, so he wondered what that was all about.

Jim gave Gene a couple of books about Christianity and said he'd like to talk to him after he had a chance to go through them. Gene did read through the books, which prompted questions about what it meant to have a personal relationship with Christ. He also confided how lonely he was without Rhonda and his family on the other side of the country.

The chaplain and player formed a bond, and Gene said that the chaplain's care and concern impacted him in a great way. "With Jim, it started with a relationship between us before he talked about what a spiritual relationship with

Christ was all about. His love and concern for me impacted my life in a mighty way."

And then one day, Jim presented the simple message of the Gospel—that Jesus Christ came on this earth to die for our sins and whoever believes in Him will have eternal life. Gene prayed to receive Christ into his heart and became a Christian. "It was a natural consequence of what God was working on in my heart at that time," he said.

Meanwhile, on the tennis court, Gene earned a spot in the starting lineup his freshman year, playing No. 4 on a talented team that would bring home a back-to-back NCAA Championship to Stanford.

He kept in touch with Rhonda during long, way-too-expensive phone calls back to the East Coast, describing every step of the spiritual journey he was on. He sent his girlfriend the books that Jim had asked him to read, which inspired even deeper discussions about Christianity and eternity between the young couple.

Rhonda was Jewish, having been raised by parents who rarely attended synagogue or talked about Jewish traditions. When Gene and Rhonda started dating in high school, there were some concerns from her parents about the match. After all, Gene was a Gentile, and she came from a Jewish heritage. Yet their relationship had survived a move during high school, all the weekends Gene was gone playing junior tournaments, as well as the coast-to-coast separation from attending Stanford University in the San Francisco Bay Area.

When Rhonda flew out to the West Coast one weekend to see Gene, the two of them met with Jim Stump to talk about spiritual matters. It turned out that Rhonda was on a quest to know God as well, and she became a Christian six months after Gene prayed to receive Christ with the Stanford chaplain.

She eventually told her parents that she became a believer in *Yeshua Ha Mashiach* — Jesus the Messiah. Their attitude was *If you want to believe in something, why don't you believe in the Jewish faith?* Yet Rhonda believed that Christ, the Messiah, had already come and died on a cross for her, which is why she made a bold decision to follow Him.

Rhonda's parents eventually came around and accepted what their daughter had done — but other family members were not so forgiving and stopped talking to her.

Smart Cookie

Gene turned pro in 1976 at the age of twenty, having entered Stanford at the age of seventeen and graduating in three years. Although he didn't win the NCAA singles championships, he was one of the top collegiate players in the country and eager to follow his brother, Sandy, into the pro ranks.

Gene was an oddity on the circuit, one of two players who played with two hands on the backhand *and* forehand side. He did not play with two forehands, but he used lots of wrist and flicked his share of shots. He placed his dominant hand — the right — on top of his left hand, which gripped the base of the racket. When he served or volleyed, however, he moved his right-hand to the base of the racket and hit those shots one-handed.

The pioneer of using both hands off both wings was Pancho Segura, the bandy-legged Ecuadorian who toured with Jack Kramer and Bobby Riggs back in the early days of pro tennis in the 1950s. When Gene turned pro, only one other player of note was playing with two hands on both sides. That was Frew McMillan, the South African doubles specialist fourteen years older on the tail end of his career.

Gene barely hung on during his rookie season. The ATP Tour had just started using computer rankings, and Gene had earned enough points—from playing professional tournaments as an amateur during his junior and senior years at Stanford—to be ranked No. 46. A string of first- and second-round losses, however, quickly dropped him to No. 148, which meant he was relegated to tennis' lowest-rung tournaments, playing for $1,000 winner's paychecks. He earned $17,000 his first year out in 1976, just enough to cover his expenses.

His game continued to flounder in 1977 until he did two things:

1. Marry Rhonda, his best friend who became a travel companion to combat the loneliness of tour life.

2. Change rackets from a small-head traditional wood racket to the over-sized Prince Graphite.

If you've ever watched film of points played from the pros in the 1960s or early 1970s, it looks like they are playing in slow-motion compared to the concussive groundstroking that's the calling card of today's modern game. There's a reason for that—the old Jack Kramer and Dunlop wooden rackets couldn't put that much pop on the ball back in the day. The introduction of the Prince Graphite racket in 1977, however, jump-started a revolution in racket technology that would pick up steam during the 1980s and 1990s.

The year 1977 was the Wimbledon's centennial year, and rackets hadn't changed much in 100 years. They were generally wooden—the notable exception being the steel Wilson T2000 brandished by Jimmy Connors—and had a hitting surface of 78 square inches. The Prince Graphite, however, had a head size measuring 110 square inches, which was a 40 percent increase. Tennis purists snickered, calling the Prince a "frying pan" and a racket for weekend hackers, but the huge sweet spot and greatly increased power allowed Gene to level the playing surface against taller, more muscular opponents.

Armed with a revolutionary racket, Gene played with even more variety on the court, and Sandy always said that he never hit two balls the same. His against-the-grain method of playing tennis made him every player's nightmare because his opponents were used to competing against players who consistently hit the ball hard and deep—the essence of the modern game. When they came up against Gene, however, they were thrown off their rhythm.

Gene, who wasn't blessed with a powerful body, did have a powerful mind that he used to disrupt and unnerve his opponents. How did he do that? By dishing up a variety of spins and changing the speed of the ball. To him, tennis wasn't all about hitting the ball hard and deep, although Gene could play like that if the occasion warranted itself. Tennis was about varying the tempo—moving the player side to side along the baseline for several shots, lulling him into a rhythm, and then feathering a drop shot over the net or hitting behind him. I saw dozens of losing players leave the court looking befuddled after shaking hands with Gene and congratulating him for his victory. It had to be frustrating to play someone who disarms you on the tennis court, but that's what Gene did.

I experienced some of that frustration myself. I can remember going bowling with Gene and having a really good game—like scoring a 180. Gene would bowl 200. Then we'd play Ping Pong, and he'd beat me 21-2. I knew better than to ever try out-eating him.

His smorgasbord of strokes and angles lifted him to No. 4 in the world at the end of the 1980 season. The three players ranked higher were all Hall of Famers: Bjorn Borg, John McEnroe, and Jimmy Connors. Looking back, this was the heyday of tennis. The Top 20 players didn't make the big prize money like they do today, but in many ways they made more money from clothing deals, exhibitions, and endorsement contracts. Gene proved that he was smart *off* the court by investing wisely and cautiously, so he did well for himself and his family.

Gene won 14 singles titles during a nine-year pro career and probably wished he did better in the Grand Slams, where his best results were two quarterfinal appearances at Wimbledon and two quarterfinal finishes at the U.S Open.

They didn't break the mold when Gene left the game in 1985. A year later, twelve-year-old Monica Seles and her parents, Károly and Eszter, moved from Yugoslavia to the United States to train at the Nick Bollettieri Tennis Academy in Florida. The parents sought out Gene's father to talk to him about the pros and cons of Monica continuing to belt two-handed forehands and backhands. The fact that Alex Mayer and Monica's parents came from the same region of Yugoslavia, could converse in Serbo-Croatian language, and knew of Gene's successful career hitting with both hands convinced the Seleses that they were on the right course. Monica won nine Grand Slam titles, but we'll never know if she could have become the greatest women's tennis player ever because of the 1993 on-court stabbing incident in which a crazed fan plunged a nine-inch-long knife into her back.

As for the men's side, diminutive Frenchman Fabrice Santoro—who enjoyed a long and successful pro career from 1989 to 2010—was called "The Magician" for the way he waved his racket like a wand. The French Federation sought out Gene to coach the two-handed Santoro when he was eighteen years old, figuring who could better teach the intricacies — and possibilities — of playing with two hands than the virtuoso himself? Gene worked with Fabrice for two years, laying the foundation for a long, successful career that ended in 2010 at the age of thirty-seven.

Today, the only active player of note hitting with two hands is Marion Bartoli, another French player.

A Closing Thought

I'm indebted to Gene because the year before he started his meteoric rise to the top echelons of tennis in 1980, he was part of the small cadre of players who met me at the T Bar M Ranch outside San Antonio, Texas, and asked me to travel on the tour.

When I spoke with Gene for this book, he wanted to say this about his time playing professional tennis:

"The tour was an abnormal life for Rhonda and me, and it was hard to maintain regular prayer and Bible study time. Having you out there, Fritz, helped me grow in God in an atmosphere geared to draw you away from God. It would have been incredibly difficult for me not to be overwhelmed by the temptations and struggles of life on the tour without your ministry. Sure, we had excitement and financial rewards while I was playing, but what I'm most thankful for is that I did not go through all that apart from Him."

These days, Gene is working with junior players on Long Island in New York. He and Rhonda are parents of two adult children, Jared and Sarah. Jared works in the financial world on Wall Street, and Sarah is working for a shipping company on Long Island.

Nduka "Duke" Odizor engages the audience during the
Wimbledon outreach in London.

6
NDUKA ODIZOR

The Duke of Tennis

I had never seen something like that happen before at a tennis tournament. In early June 1990, I was in the Dutch town of 's-Hertogenbosch—try saying that five times consecutively—some eighty kilometers south of Amsterdam. This was the site of a grass-court event to be staged two weeks before the start of Wimbledon, a time when the players were adjusting from the red clay of Roland Garros to the slick, cushiony feel of grass courts.

I was leaning against the fence watching one of my favorite players, Nduka Odizor, warm up on the practice court. All the guys in the locker room called him "Duke," a nickname that seemed to fit. Then the press took things one step further by referring to this regal, ebony player from Nigeria as the "Duke of Odizor."

Before I tell you what happened in 's-Hertogenbosch that afternoon, you need to understand just how far Nduka had traveled to become a professional tennis player. Born in Lagos, Nigeria, Duke grew up in a shantytown filled with despair and little hope. His parents got him a job as a ball boy at the Ikoyi Tennis Club, whose membership was made up of wealthy British expats. He ran around the court chasing balls, earning a few shillings to supplement the family income. "I got a dollar a month, but that was sufficient to subsidize my parent's income for buying food for the entire month," Duke told me.

When Duke was twelve years old, Stan Smith and Arthur Ashe toured Nigeria on a goodwill trip sponsored by the U.S. State Department. America's top two players gave tennis clinics to introduce the game to African youngsters, many of whom had never seen a tennis racket before. Duke showed up gripping a board carved from a broken table. There were no strings — just a flat wooden surface.

Duke was a fun-loving kid with a quick smile, and the Ikoyi Club members adopted him as one of their own. They gave him a real racket, and he began playing seriously when he was fourteen years old. Two years later, Robert Wren, a University of Houston professor who was guest lecturing at the University of Lagos, dropped by the club for a hit. Duke was the only player around, so the two rallied for hours in the African heat.

By now, Duke was showing some serious game, and Wren was impressed with the raw talent he saw. He asked Duke if he would be interested in going to America, where he could attend college and play tennis. "I'll sponsor you," said the professor. That act of kindness changed the direction of Nduka's life.

Professor Wren followed through on his promise, and Nduka arrived in the United States in 1977 at the age of eighteen to attend the University of Houston. If the story of a Nigerian athlete playing sports at the University of Houston sounds familiar to you, then it's because Duke paved the way for his countryman, seven-footer Hakeem (The Dream) Olajuwon, to play basketball at the University of Houston from 1981-1984.

Duke thrived on the upgrade of competition. In fact, he improved so quickly that he rapidly became one of the best collegiate players in the country. He was whipping players like Kevin Curran, who were turning pro and telling Duke that he should join them on the tour. His quickness was unreal, and his ball-striking ability was off the charts. He just needed some big-match experience.

Duke's journey of faith matched his journey to the United States. He grew up attending a Catholic parochial school in Nigeria, wearing a uniform of a starched white shirt and dark blue pants, but he never really understood that Christ had died on a cross for him so that he could actually know God and have eternal life. At one point Duke wanted to become a priest, but then someone explained what the word "celibacy" meant, and Nduka said that wasn't for him.

Like Stan Smith, he heard the gospel preached during his sophomore year at the University of Houston. He accepted Jesus into his heart with great joy, and people often said he was the happiest man around. His cheerfulness was infectious.

He played like a happy person on the court. Many players are grumpy during their matches, showing their irritation when they fall behind, get a bad line call, or hear the umpire overrule one of their winning shots. Not Duke. He played tennis with the same sort of joyfulness that runner Eric Liddell displayed in the film, *Chariots of Fire*, when he said, "I believe God made me for a purpose, but he also made me run fast. And when I run, I feel His pleasure."

Duke felt that same pleasure hitting a tennis ball and was

grateful just for the chance to play. There was no Gloomy Gus in Nduka.

"I didn't take anything on the tennis court personally because when I came to America, it was a blessing from God," he said. "An American person might see this differently, but I didn't. The lifespan in Nigeria at that time was around twenty-five years, so that was another blessing. I didn't have to live in a hut that leaked when it rained. I got to drive in a car and turn lights on when I stepped into a home. Praise God that I didn't need a kerosene lamp to see in the dark as in my home country. So everything I did, every match I played, wasn't that big a deal to me. To be alive and see another day was a success."

Turning Pro

Duke was a three-time All-American at the University of Houston and was voted the school's Athlete of the Year in 1981. He also ran on the track team when the meets fit into his schedule. He graduated with a marketing degree.

His tennis buddies had told him that he should leave school and turn pro after his junior year, but Duke wanted to stay until he graduated. "With an education, you have a good chance of getting a decent job," he reasoned.

When his college eligibility was up, he played Challenger events and quickly worked his way up the ATP Tour rankings and solidly into the Top 100. Now he was playing guys he had seen on television. He experienced some notoriety because he was one of a handful of black players on the tour in the 1980s. There were probably a half-dozen African and African-American players thirty years ago. The most notable black player was Yannick Noah, who was discovered in 1971 by Arthur Ashe during the *same* goodwill tour of Africa with Stan Smith and other American players.

At the time, eleven-year-old Yannick was given a chance to play with Ashe while the American troupe stopped in the former French colony of Cameroon. The precocious Yannick aced the U.S. Open champion and matched him rally for rally, which impressed Arthur. Upon his return to the U.S., Ashe contacted Philippe Chatrier, head of the French Tennis Federation, and told him he spotted a young player with off-the-chart talent. Chatrier invited Yannick to attend a special tennis academy in Nice, France, and twelve years later, Yannick was the No. 1 player in France and winner of the 1983 French Open.

Nduka would never win a Grand Slam, but he acquitted himself well on the tour, usually ranking in the Top 50. What I appreciated about him was his great attitude and how he became a regular fixture at our weekly Bible studies. I could always count on him to be there.

Because of our close relationship, I made sure that I watched Duke play his matches. Two high-profile duels stick in my mind.

The first happened at the 1987 Cincinnati event when Duke was playing Jimmy Connors, who was nearly thirty-five years old but *still* ranked No. 4 in the world.

Duke had a good tournament, winning three matches to make the quarterfinals. Jimbo raced out to a 6-1, 4-1 lead, but Duke battled back and forced a second-set tiebreaker, which he won. That turnaround set Connors in a bad mood.

The world's former No. 1 worked himself to a 5-3 lead and was serving for the match. On break point, though, Duke thought he clipped the line with a winning forehand, but the ball was called out. He appealed to the chair umpire, who wasn't going to overrule the call. Nduka continued to press his case, which got the crowd riled up.

Jimmy, who was used to being the center of attention, reached into his pocket for a tennis ball. He hit the ball straight up into the air, probably thirty feet—and caught the ball with his steel T2000 racket before it hit the ground. The next one was higher—forty feet. Jimmy fielded that pop-up cleanly, "catching" the ball on his strings like Willie Mays making a basket catch. The next ball went fifty feet in the air with another clean catch. The amused audience egged Jimmy to hit the next ball higher.

Then Duke smacked the ball into the air, but it sailed on him and bounced into the grandstands.

"Point penalty, Odizor," the chair umpire intoned into the microphone.

"What!" Duke approached the umpire for an explanation.

"You violently hit the ball. Point penalty."

Unnerved, Duke lost the next game and the match, 6-1, 6-7, 6-3.

At the Lipton tournament in Key Biscayne, Florida, I witnessed another miscarriage of justice. Duke was playing John McEnroe at a time when the New Yorker was ruling the game. An "upset special" was in the wind as Duke really took it to McEnroe, working himself into a position where the Nigerian was serving for the match.

The two had some history. At the 1985 Australian Open, Duke was serving so big on the grass courts that McEnroe moved fifteen feet behind the baseline, *really* far back for the serve. So Duke popped in an underhanded serve, which easily bounced twice before McEnroe could move up and hit the return. The unlikely ace ticked off McEnroe, who dialed up the intensity.

During the changeover at the Lipton tournament, when Duke was serving for the match, McEnroe said he had an injury and asked for the trainer. Well, it took a few minutes to round up someone to attend to McEnroe. He massaged some of Mac's leg muscles and applied ointment. When the umpire asked for a report, the trainer said he could find no injury. McEnroe, of course, contended that he was hurt, and the argument between him and the umpire got more heated. The umpire ordering McEnroe to play, but Mac said he wasn't ready. Of course, all this was done to throw off his opponent who was waiting to serve for the match.

Finally, the chair umpire had had enough. "Game, set, and match, Odizor," he announced, awarding a default to Duke of Odizor.

You can imagine the controversy that ensued. The tournament didn't want to lose its No. 1 seed and top draw. In one of the most pronounced instances of tennis injustice that I ever saw, the *following day* tournament organizers fired the umpire, overturned his decision, and announced that McEnroe was the winner of the match. I don't know how that could be done in tennis, but it happened. I was upset because that ruling cost Duke prize money and bonus points for defeating a top-ranked player.

I remember Duke not being bothered that much. I don't mean to insinuate that he didn't care, but he had a different perspective on life. He had already *won* because he had accepted Jesus Christ as his Savior. Knowing Christ and reading the Bible gave him an eternal perspective on winning and losing and treating others as he would want to be treated. Of course he experienced racism, growing up in Nigeria and making his home in the United States, but he never looked to settle any scores, even when others didn't want much to do with him. I saw him ask different players if they wanted to practice with him, and their first response was often no. But a few days later, or a week or two later, I'd see Duke exchanging groundstrokes with the player who turned him down. He won people over to him and had that sort of effect on players.

Duke had a lot of Christian friends on the tour. He was the type of leader who made sure they all hung out together and were involved in each other's lives. They held each other mutually accountable for their actions on and off the court. When the men's tour played at the same venue as the women—like at the four Grand Slams—he reached out to Christians in the women's game. If a church asked him to speak and share his faith, he was there, like the time when he and African-American player Camille Benjamin spoke together at a black church in Brixton, Great Britain, on the Sunday before the start of Wimbledon.

Wimbledon was the site of perhaps his greatest victory. In the first round of the 1983 championships, he was told that he would be playing the great Guillermo Vilas on Centre Court. Vilas was never known as a great grass court player, but he was a two-time winner of the Australian Open, which was played on grass in the late 1970s. (He was also a single-time champion of the U.S. Open and French Open.)

Duke had never played on Centre Court before. He was ranked a lowly No. 82 in the world and playing in only his second Wimbledon. He lost the first two sets and extended the third into a tiebreaker. He saved a match point, took the third set, and won the fourth and fifth sets playing brilliant tennis, using the topspin lob to perfection.

The upset was the talk of Wimbledon that day, and the Fleet Street reporters in the press room wanted an explanation. "At first before I went out to Centre Court, I thought I'd be nervous," he said. "Amazingly, I was not."

Duke Odizor traveled a long way to get from Lagos, Nigeria, to Centre Court at Wimbledon.

One of the most difficult things for a lower-ranked player is to follow an upset with a victory. This time, there was no let down. Duke defeated Peter Fleming and Loïc Courteau to reach the Round of 16, where New Zealander Chris Lewis was waiting for him. The match was freighted with heavy importance for both players, who were unseeded and hungry to make a breakthrough. At this Wimbledon match, Lewis handled the occasion better, winning handily in three straight sets. In fact, the New Zealander rode the momentum all the way to the finals, where he was bowled over by John McEnroe. You have to wonder if Duke could have become the first African player to reach a Wimbledon final.

(One of the highlights of my time on the tour was when four Christian tennis players—Sandy Mayer, Mike Leach, Mel Purcell, and Nduka reached the fourth round of Wimbledon during the 1983 championships. I remember hustling around the grounds of the All England Club like Lovely Rita, the meter maid, to catch all the matches. Sandy was actually pitted against Mike Leach and defeated him easily, 6-1, 7-6, 6-1. John McEnroe got him the next round.)

Still, Duke's successes at Wimbledon and around the tennis world made him a national hero back home in Nigeria. It was said that when he went home the customs officials waved him through the line, and he never had to wait for a restaurant table or a taxi. Lagos newspapers called him "The Prince of the Niger." Because of all the attention, he said it was nice not to be recognized or bothered when he was back in the United States.

When Duke married his wife, Karen, in early 1983, he told interviewers that God was the most important thing in his life, followed by his wife and then tennis. He retired from the game in 1992 and established a tennis club in the Houston area and put his marketing degree to good use by opening an advertising agency. He and Karen also became parents to a son, Nicholas.

He also gave back to his home continent by starting a company called Swift Construction Company to build thousands of homes in Namibia, using a technology that allowed them to construct the homes in two days and cost 90 percent below traditional methods. He lent his name and time to Tennis for Africa, a charity that built hospitals and orphanages in Africa.

The Shirt Off His Back

About that other incident I described at the beginning of this chapter—the one in 's-Hertogenbosch, the Netherlands. This episode happened toward the end of Duke's career, when he had dropped down to No. 200 in the world. A low ranking like this meant that he couldn't play in any main-draw tournaments, which paid the most prize money to the players as well as offered the most ranking points. Instead, he was relegated to the qualifying tournaments.

When Duke came off the practice court that day, he over-heard his next opponent complaining to a friend that he didn't have a pair of the special grass court shoes—the ones with small round nibs on the outsoles that help the player keep his footing as he changes direction.

"It's slicker than snot out there," he said.

Duke interjected himself into the conversation.

"What size shoe do you wear?" he asked.

The player recognized Nduka and knew they would be playing each other that afternoon. "Forty-four," he replied, using the European standard. "Why do you ask?"

"Because I have a pair back at the hotel that you can use."

His opponent's face dropped in astonishment. The thought *How could anyone playing against me be so stupid?* was written all over his face.

Duke reached into his tennis bag. "Here's my hotel key. You can get them or send somebody for you."

An hour later, Duke stepped onto the court with an oppo-nent who was wearing his extra pair of grass court sneakers. Obviously, the Nigerian would have had a distinct advan-tage playing against someone without grass court shoes. He would have moved around the court like he was on roller skates.

His opponent won the first set, but then Duke turned the match around and won the final two sets to take the match. As they shook hands at the net, his opponent couldn't thank him enough.

"He was so sincere," Duke said. "He said nothing like

this had ever happened to him before. He was flabbergasted!"

I had been teaching on how the Bible tells us to "let your light shine before men." God doesn't want us to hide our light. Instead, we need to set it on a hill. I asked Duke to write about this amazing match for one of my bimonthly newsletters, and here's what he had to say:

"I am beginning to see this light materialize in my life. I can honestly say I never even considered the outcome of the match when I offered him my shoes. I just hope that this has long-lasting meaning to him . . . that he'll look back in six months or a year and maybe that will be part of bringing him to Christ."

See, I told you Nduka "Duke" Odizor was a prince of a guy!

Nduka and Karen continue to live in the Houston area where Nduka gives lessons and works in various business ventures.

On his website, he said his tennis teaching philosophy can be summed up in four points:

1. My Christian faith is evident in my tennis coaching

2. Tennis is a microcosm of life

3. Tennis should be fun and open to anyone who wants to play

4. I am the wrong coach if you expect me to yell at your kids.

Michael Chang, shown hitting a backhand at the annual indoor
tournament in Memphis, Tennessee, is the youngest male
player to win a Grand Slam tournament. He captured the 1989
French Open at the age of seventeen years, three months.

7
MICHAEL CHANG
Standing Tall for Christ

I watched a lot of tennis matches during my years on the tour, too many to count. If I had to hazard a guess, though, you can figure that I dropped in on probably ten matches a day. Multiply that number by six days a week, thirty tournaments a year, twelve seasons on the tour, and you get a grand total of roughly 21,600 matches.

I'm surprised that I haven't gone on disability for swiveling my neck so much.

I witnessed a lot of amazing duels, like the time when thirty-nine-year-old Jimmy Connors whipped up the crowd when he defeated Aaron Krickstein in a thrilling fifth-set tiebreaker at the 1991 U.S. Open. Another memorable match was watching seventeen-year-old Andre Agassi make his first splash by beating Wimbledon champion Pat Cash at the Stratton Mountain event in Vermont.

I didn't see any famous finals, however — like Borg versus McEnroe at Wimbledon or Agassi versus Sampras at the U.S. Open. I was usually headed to the next tour stop when the tournament reached the semifinal and final stage. It was important that I be there to lead the Sunday night Bible study at the new tournament.

If you were to ask me which match stood out above the rest, then I would have to say that it was a Round of 16 contest I witnessed in early June 1989. I'm talking about a titanic struggle played out between Michael Chang of Placentia, California, and Czechoslovakia's Ivan Lendl, the No. 1 player in the world, at Roland Garros' Court Central. If you're of a certain age, then you remember it well.

Just seventeen years and three months old, Michael should have been finishing up his junior year of high school, but he was a tennis prodigy who'd been out on tour since he was fifteen, having turned pro one week before his sixteenth birthday. Even though he was the French Open's fifteenth seed and had already notched some great wins, no one gave him any chance against Ivan Lendl, the no-nonsense Czech and ultimate professional who swatted away opponents like they were pests. Tennis pundits expected Lendl to exterminate Michael in three straight sets.

Some of the pre-match coverage in the newspapers talked about the "David versus Goliath" match-up between Chang and Lendl, and the metaphor fit. When boyish-looking Michael walked onto Court Central, he reminded me of a certain young shepherd boy who took on the world's most powerful and strongest man with overwhelming odds against his survival. This time around, instead of a slingshot and several smooth stones in his pouch, Michael's weapons were a Prince Graphite racket and a deep reservoir of guile.

I sat in Michael's player box on that memorable day in Paris, three or four rows above Betty Chang, Michael's mother. She traveled everywhere with her son, which could only be expected since he was just seventeen years old. He didn't even have a driver's license yet.

I'll never forget the first time I met Betty at Wimbledon the year before. She approached me and asked if I could help her find a trainer for Michael. She must have mistaken me for one of the ATP staffers. "Actually, I don't help players physically," I said.

"Then what do you do?" she asked.

"I help players spiritually on the tour."

Betty liked hearing that. She was a Christian, just like her getting-more-famous-by-the-minute son. We soon found out we had something else in common: we both attended and graduated from Malone College in Canton.

Talk about a small world.

Betty and Mike—that's what a lot of people on the tour, including myself, called Michael when he first came out—soon became regular fixtures at our weekly Bible studies. Michael told me that he had recently accepted Jesus Christ into his heart after he began reading an *NIV Student Bible* that his grandmother had given him. The Bible contained thought-provoking lessons as well as explanations about certain passages of Scripture. In a quiet moment one evening, he made a commitment to Jesus Christ as his Lord and Savior. From that day forward, he wanted to learn more about Him, live like Him, and follow Him. When Michael told his parents what he had done, they became believers in Christ as well. So did his older brother, Carl, three years his senior and a fine player in his own right.

I first heard of Michael when he was fifteen years old and won the U.S. Boys 18 Nationals at Kalamazoo, Michigan. The United States Tennis Association always awards a wildcard into the U.S. Open for the Kalamazoo winner, and Michael seized the moment. At the 1987 U.S. Open, he defeated

Australia's Paul McNamee, seventeen years his senior at thirty-two years of age, in four sets. The first-round victory made Michael the youngest male to ever win a U.S. Open match in the Open era and set off a media hullabaloo. Back then, the two mainstays of American tennis—John McEnroe and Jimmy Connors—hadn't won a Grand Slam tournament in several years.

Michael's next opponent was one of my guys—Nduka Odizor. I made sure I went out to Court 16 early for that one because the grandstands had room for only several hundred people. I noticed U.S. Davis Cup captain Tom Gorman and former players Arthur Ashe and Brian Gottfried dropped by to take a look at this Asian-American kid kicking up some dust.

Duke overwhelmed Michael the first two sets, losing just three games, but I was impressed with Michael's fighting spirit. This kid would not give up! He clawed his way back into the match, winning the next two sets. The match could have gone either way in the fifth set, but then Michael missed an easy put-away at 3-4, lost his serve, and lost the match 6-3 in the fifth. He could have won, and he knew it.

I knew it was only a matter of time before Michael was out on the tour full-time. His groundstrokes were solid, his quickness was off-the-chart, and the harder you hit, the harder he hit. The kid was a great counter-puncher. You took the net on him at your peril.

He kept winning after he turned pro the following spring and made amazing strides in the rankings, jumping from No. 163 to the world's Top 20 in just one year. What I liked about Michael was that he was rapidly growing in his faith as well. Not only was he willing to talk about his faith in Jesus Christ to the media, but he *wanted* to. It was simply the overflow of everything going on inside of him.

From everything I saw, from the across-the-table conversations I had with him to the questions he asked in our Bible studies, this likeable teen was the real deal. I could tell he was reading his Bible from the discussions we had, and I knew he felt close to the Lord.

Back in the City of Light

I remember several things about the Lendl match at the 1989 French Open. First, he started out like he did against the Duke of Odizor — by losing the first two sets. Now, when you lose two long 4-6, 4-6 sets on clay and have nothing to show for two hours of herculean effort, it's practically impossible to will the mind back into the match. The losing player's resistance wavers a bit, and the next thing he knows, he's shaking hands at the net and congratulating the winner. I'd seen it happen hundreds of times.

Michael's resolve didn't seem to weaken, at least from my vantage point. Betty was sitting near José Higueras, the great Spanish clay courter who was Michael's coach, as well as his agent, Jeff Austin. We were just beyond the baseline overlooking the court.

Michael kept battling Ivan during the third set with long energy-sapping rallies. He played like his purpose was to win a set before Lendl vanquished him, but everyone knew that if Michael won a set, then he was back in the match.

Well, Michael did claim the third set, 6-3, with a late break. It was the first set that Lendl had lost in the tournament, and he wasn't a happy camper. Now he was being taken to a fourth set against an opponent who ran like a rabbit and didn't miss a ball. I'm sure the twenty-nine-old veteran wanted to get off that court.

Lendl ratcheted up the pressure. He had break points in the first, fifth, seventh, and ninth games of the fourth set, but each time he failed to convert because Michael presented him with an impenetrable wall. Impatience set in on Lendl's side of the net. I could hear the Czech muttering under his breath, especially after another shot by Michael swiped the line.

Then Lendl had a problem with the clay court. Ivan wasn't liking some of the bounces he was getting, so he took a few swipes at the *terre battue* with his racket, much like Hank Pfister did on the grass courts of Wimbledon. He complained about line calls, prompting umpire Richard Ings to bound out of the chair to inspect several marks, which set off deafening whistles from the crowd. When the French tennis fans get on your case, they can make your life miserable and lift the opposing player to new heights.

After Michael rode the crowd's support to take the fourth set, 6-3, the energy level in our player's box reached into the heavens. Even though the match was even, I don't think any of us—except for Betty, of course—believed Michael could outlast the mighty Lendl, known as just about the fittest player on the tour. The guy did not crack, as the French commentators liked to say.

Cramps latched on to Michael's legs, and several times it looked like he couldn't go any further. Sometimes all he could do was hit moonballs to pace himself. During changeovers, he ate bananas and didn't sit down, lest the cramping get worse. But he gritted his teeth and hung in there. The tension was incredible in his player's box.

Two points changed the direction of Michael's life, and they get replayed every time there's a feature story on Michael that revisits his career. The first happened when Michael was serving at 4-3 in the fifth set, up a break but down 15-30 in the game. All of us in his box knew the stakes: if Lendl won the point, he'd probably win the game to level the match at 4-4. His powerful serve would take him to a 5-4 lead, and tremendous pressure would fall on Michael's shoulders to stay in the match.

In other words, this was a huge point that could turn the match either way.

I don't know why Michael served underhand at 15-30. I had never seen a player serve underhand in all the thousands of matches I had observed over the years — and none since then. But it wasn't *exactly* an underhand serve, as many have called it over the years. What Michael did was this: instead of tossing the ball into air and hitting it with a service motion, he let the ball drop out of his hand. Then he sideswiped the ball, which put sidespin on the ball.

The underhand serve floated through the air at half the normal speed of his second serve. Lendl reacted a split-second late and advanced on the ball. The sidespin caused the ball to bounce into his body. Instead of whacking a winner on such a slow serve, Ivan had to push the ball into Michael's forehand court without much on the return. Michael wound up and ripped a forehand up the line, which clipped the net and ricocheted off Ivan's outstretched racket at the net.

Thirty-all!

You could have fried an egg on Lendl's generous red forehead. He was ticked, but he didn't say anything. I think he knew he had been had by a serve that people would remember for decades to come.

Michael went on to win the next two points to consolidate his break and take a 5-3 lead. With the French crowd yelling "Allez, allez," Michael seized the moment and worked Ivan into a 15-40 hole, double-match point.

Michael had one more trick up his sleeve. After Ivan faulted on the first serve, he crept in to within three or four feet of the service line—a tactic, he said afterward, that he employed in his junior matches to distract his opponent. Perfectly legal, as long as you don't wave your racket.

Lendl appealed to the umpire Richard Ings, who remained mute. Perhaps fearing the wrath of the French crowd, Lendl thought better of making a scene. He went through his familiar service motion. The ball clipped the net and bounced two feet long, and our box and Court Central erupted in joy.

Goliath had been slain.

At the press conference afterward, dozens of reporters asked Michael how and why he won.

"Because the Lord Jesus gave me strength," he replied.

The American reporters in the room were well familiar with Michael's faith since he rarely did *not* talk about Christ in his interviews. But to the secular European press corps in the room, this was over the top.

I heard that one reporter asked him, "Did God hit your serve?" in reference to the surprise underhand attempt in the fifth set.

All Michael could do was smile. Of course God didn't hit his serve. Besides, I like to think that if God did hit one of Michael's serves for him, no one would ever see it.

Michael went on to win the French Open, defeating Sweden's Stefan Edberg to become the youngest-ever male to win a Grand Slam singles championship. When he was handed a microphone to address the French crowd after the trophy presentation, he said, "I want to thank the Lord Jesus Christ, because without Him, I am nothing."

Now it was Michael's turn to hear the jeers and whistles

from the fickle French. They let him have it pretty good. Little did Michael know that his bold witness for Christ would attract the attention of one of his major sponsors, and they would become uncomfortable with all his God talk.

Meeting a Legend

Three weeks later, I was walking on the streets of London with Michael and Betty, who were still reeling from all the attention that Michael's unlikely victory had generated.

Betty said that one of his major sponsors had asked Michael not to be so bold about his faith — to back off a bit so that he would not become a polarizing sports figure. They were both clearly torn by this turn of events. How could they not talk about what the Lord had done in their lives?

I didn't know what to say except to say that we needed to pray about this and ask for the Lord's direction.

Back at the player's hotel, Betty handed me a fistful of telephone messages and a sack of mail. She wanted me to screen them for her and Michael.

One of the phone messages caught my attention. The call was from Maury Scobee of the Billy Graham Evangelistic Association. That was interesting. I had heard that Billy Graham was in London for a series of preaching events that would be heard by more than 800,000 people and broadcast to millions around the world.

I called Maury and explained who I was and why I was calling on behalf of Michael. "How can I help you?" I asked.

Maury asked me a few questions about what I did, so I explained that I held Bible studies, organized housing, and formed relationships with players, all with an eye for helping the players grow in their faith. Then Maury asked me to describe what Michael was like, and I talked about the courage he'd shown in talking about Christ every time a microphone was thrust under his chin. I also brought Maury up to date on all the craziness that had happened since Michael's unlikely victory in Paris.

"Would you be available for dinner tonight?" Maury asked.

"Sure," I replied. "Where would you like to meet?"

"Actually, I was wondering if you'd be available for dinner tonight with Dr. Graham and his wife, Ruth," he said.

I nearly dropped the phone. The thought of having dinner with the greatest evangelist of the 20th century blew my mind.

So I met Billy and Ruth Graham at their hotel for dinner, where we were escorted to a private dining salon. It feels funny writing this, but I never felt so comfortable in my life. They were talking to me like we were old friends. Billy enjoyed hearing my story about how I came to Christ through one of his movies — *Time to Run* — when I was a student at Malone College.

Dr. Graham followed sports — he liked to play golf — and he was full of questions about Michael Chang. What was he like? Was he getting flack for being outspoken about Christ?

Actually, he was, I said, and I explained the situation with one of his sponsors.

"I would like to meet this young man," Billy said.

Ruth added that she really wanted to meet the Chang family because she had been born and raised in China for the first seventeen years of her life. Her father had been a medical missionary in the eastern Chinese province of Northern Kiangsu, and coming of age in China had left her with indelible love for the Chinese people.

We set up a time during the middle Sunday of

Wimbledon for the Changs to meet Billy and Ruth Graham at their hotel. Joe and Carl hopped on a plane in Los Angeles to be there. As Michael wrote in his autobiography, *Holding Serve*, he had an odd sensation that this kindly giant of the Christian faith could look right into his heart and see any unconfessed sins residing there. Dr. Graham encouraged Michael to grow in his walk with Christ and stay close to Him.

Michael heard those words, and I saw this special tennis player grow and mature in his faith in a way that played out on and off the court. Michael got more out of his talent than anyone I ever saw on the men's tour. His serve got better each year. Every facet of his game improved each year. He had oodles of determination, and it showed.

Eventually, over the next couple of years, Team Chang became the support team around Michael. His brother, Carl, became his coach, and his parents, Joe and Betty, remained close and highly involved. We stopped seeing him at our weekly Bible studies, but I knew he was getting spiritually fed and that he was regularly reading his Bible. We remained quite friendly to each other.

Three years after Michael won the French Open, I left the tour for family reasons of my own at the end of the 1992 season. Michael's best years were ahead of him, and he would eventually rise to No. 2 in the world. He would have become No. 1 in the world if he had beaten an old rival, Pete Sampras, in the finals of the 1996 U.S. Open, but he came up short.

He retired from the game in 2003 at the U.S. Open, and one of the first things he did was take Bible classes at Biola University, a Christian college near his hometown in the Orange County region of Southern California. He coached a couple of players on the tour, including the female Chinese player, Peng Shuai. Then he met a Chinese-American player who was a two-time NCAA champion out of Stanford University, Amber Liu. Attracted by her looks and her deep faith in Christ, Michael and Amber fell in love and were married in October 2008. They have an eighteen-month-old daughter, Lani, and make their home in Orange County.

Today, you can occasionally see Michael back on court playing in "senior" tennis events with the likes of Andre Agassi, Pete Sampras, Jim Courier, and John McEnroe. His charitable foundation, the Chang Family Foundation, has launched the Christian Sports League in Seattle (where Michael lived for a period of time toward the latter end of his playing career) and Orange County. The Christian Sports League is a vehicle for local churches and organizations to share the Gospel through organized and competitive sports like volleyball, basketball, and tennis tournaments.

It's hard to believe that Michael is forty years old, which goes to show how quickly time flies.

But thanks, Michael, for the memories.

We'll always have Paris.

With his blue jeans tennis shorts and long, frosted hair,
Andre Agassi swept the tennis world off its feet during
his breakthrough year in 1988.

8
ANDRE AGASSI
A Mystery Wrapped Inside a Two-Handed Enigma

There are many things I could say about Andre Agassi because for nearly three years, at the start of his long and meteoric career, we spent a lot of time together. We shared intimate discussions about things that matter most in life — Jesus Christ, eternity in heaven, and our role as Christians — and I did my best to disciple him. There are only a few things that I feel at liberty to discuss, however, and we'll have to keep things that way.

I first heard about Andre sometime in the spring of 1986. I was hanging out at a satellite tournament in Waco, Texas, making myself available to young, aspiring pros trying to earn enough ranking points to graduate to the ATP tour. Although it may sound like I globe-trotted around the world in this book, traveling to one famous tournament after another, I actually spent a fair amount of my time in tennis' minor leagues attending either satellite or qualifying tournaments. I found that the players at this level were more open to conversations about life and faith, less self-protective, and more available to hang out, which is how relationships are built.

At Waco, the sun slipped under the horizon at dusk, and you should have seen the mosquitoes and all sorts of creepy bugs come out. They swarmed like locusts over the tournament site, causing people to seek shelter inside the clubhouse. So many mosquitoes were attracted to the lights that the players couldn't see the ball very well, so the evening matches were suspended. Can you believe that? Wild!

I was hanging out inside the tennis club when a young player in the satellite tournament made eye contact with me and introduced himself. He said his name was Phil Agassi. I shook his hand and introduced myself as well, but I didn't say anything about being a tennis chaplain. I leaned back and listened to his mile-a-minute monologue, including his declaration that his little brother was going to be a famous tennis player.

"Just you wait," Phil said. "He's going to be winning Slams some day."

I admired Phil's confidence in his brother, but at the same time, I knew what the reality was. Only a handful of tennis players were ever special enough to win Grand Slam tournaments and capture fame and fortune.

"What's his name?" I asked, thinking I'd file his name away for future reference.

"Andre . . . Andre Agassi," Phil said.

"How old is he?"

"Sixteen. I'm telling you, he's been at Bollettieri's for several years, and he's cleaning everyone's clock down there."

Phil was referring to a tennis academy run by a former Marine named Nick Bollettieri. Tennis academies were where junior players come to develop their games from sunup to sundown—eat, sleep, and dream tennis. The harsh regimen fortified young players like boot camp toughened

In 1988, while at a tournament in Seoul, South Korea, I walked around
the Itaewon shopping district before the Summer Olympics
with Andre Agassi (left) and his brother, Phil.

up a barracks full of raw recruits.

Three or four months later, I was in Stratton Mountain,
Vermont, for one of the ATP's main tour events. I was relax-
ing in the outdoor Jacuzzi at the player's hotel, enjoying the
setting sun, when Phil and Andre joined me in the hot tub.

Phil remembered meeting me in Waco, and someone
must have told him about my tour chaplaincy because Andre
immediately started peppering me with questions about
God:

• *What do you believe about the Bible?*

- *Is the Bible true?*
- *What do you think of all the evil in the world?*

I told Andre that I did believe the Bible was true. I quickly added that every word in the Bible could mean something very important in your life because all Scripture is the inspired Word of God.

Andre seemed to like what I had to say, and when he asked what Christianity was all about, I told him how Jesus walked this Earth for thirty-three years, and when he died on a cross, He took the sins of men with Him and rose again from the dead so that we could have eternal life with Him.

He pressed me on why there seemed to be evil everywhere, and I replied that it was because there was sin in the world. "But like it says in the Bible, good things overcome evil things eventually. But that doesn't mean that Christians won't have bad things happen, like getting cancer or being in a horrific auto accident. It doesn't matter what kind of good life you live, bad things can happen to you."

"Fritz, I'd like to talk to you again," Andre said, as he stepped out of the Jacuzzi. And that was the start of our relationship as well as our friendship.

When I saw him play for the first time at Stratton Mountain, I could see why Phil told me that his brother was going to be famous some day. He was sixteen years old with a two-tone mullet (blond highlights up top, brown hair below) who hit big off the ground for someone as thin as a whippet. The kid was a ball-striker with quite a developed game for someone so young.

Andre raised some eyebrows when he beat Tim Mayotte and Scott Davis, two highly ranked American players, in the early rounds. John McEnroe, who was still at the height of his powers in the mid-1980s, finally subdued the precocious talent in the quarterfinals. His ranking rose from No. 208 to No. 101.

Then Andre hit a speed bump in the summer of 1987, when he was seventeen and the wild cards had run out. Andre lost in the qualifications of a tour stop in Washington, D.C., to a player far below his talent. It was the latest of a long list of matches that had slipped from his grasp, and Andre lost it, totally lost it.

Seconds after shaking hands, he grabbed his racket bag and hightailed it out of the tournament site. Phil and I hustled to keep up with him.

He was beside himself, nearly in tears. He couldn't beat anybody, no matter how hard he tried. The next thing I know, Andre unzipped his racket bag and flung two rackets into a nearby lake. I definitely remember the splash of water.

"I'm quitting this game," Andre wailed.

"Don't quit, Andre," I said. "God doesn't care if you won or lost. He just cares if you gave it your best. You've got far too much talent to stop now. Just give Him your tennis, as well as your results."

Eventually, Andre got some new rackets (he played with the Prince Graphite in those days), and he received a wild card into Stratton Mountain again because of his surprising quarterfinal result the year previously.

Since trying to win on his own strength wasn't getting him anywhere, he told me that he vowed to play his first-round match against Luke Jensen without caring who won the points. Well, there's a fine line between playing "free" and competing with everything you have.

Andre lost the first set. He was down a break, 3-1, in the second when Luke hit a big winner and did a demonstrative fist pump.

Fast food stop: from the left, Robin's sister, Shelby and Donna; Andre Agassi; Robin and me; Phil Agassi; and Debbie and David Pate.

Something clicked in Andre. It was like he realized that he was blessed with this abundance of talent, and he had an obligation to the Lord to make the most of it. He smoked Jensen in the second and third sets, and then it was like Andre was a different player.

Then I was courtside when he played Pat Cash, the Australian serve-and-volleyer who had surprised the tennis world when he won Wimbledon the previous month by defeating Ivan Lendl. Andre went toe-to-toe with Cash and didn't give an inch, pulling out a 7-6, 7-6 victory and winning the tiebreakers 10-8 and 8-6. I thought I was going to chew every fingernail off.

Andre was on his way. He pushed Ivan Lendl to three sets in the semifinals before losing, prompting the dour Czech to famously remark that Andre was nothing more than a "haircut and a forehand."

And then Andre had his breakout year in 1988, when he stormed the tennis world and shot up to No. 4 in the world. It's hard to explain how bright the spotlight was on Andre, but he was the talk of the sporting world — an eighteen-year-old phenom with long, frosted hair and a diamond stud in one ear.

Andre said in interviews that he was a believer, and in those early days, he even brought his Bible to sit-down meetings with the press. He was quite vocal about his faith, so much so that reporters routinely used the phrase "born-again Christian" to describe him.

As word seeped through the culture that a "born-again Christian" was one of the most exciting tennis personalities in the world, Christian organizations asked him to come speak at their annual fundraiser or charity events.

Andre and Phil asked me to handle the speaking requests from Christian organizations as well as interviews with Christian magazines and radio programs. My standard answer was that Andre would love to come, but his schedule was too busy, which was true. But there was another reason, and it was that Andre was not ready. He was eighteen, nineteen years old, still young in his faith. He was not ready to get up before an audience and share his testimony or what God was teaching him. He needed time to mature in the Lord.

I remember explaining this to one Christian organization that was persistent in trying to get Andre to come to some big event they were staging. When I told them that Andre wasn't ready to speak before an audience, I was told, "Well, Andre can just stand on the stage, and he won't have to say a thing." I failed to see how that would advance the

Kingdom, having Andre stand there like a mannequin.

During our time together, I made some awesome memories. One time, I went to Andre's house in Las Vegas. I saw the multiple ball machines set up on his backyard court, and he explained how his father had rigged them up to fire at him like a machine gun nest. I saw a collection of the hottest cars parked in the driveway—including a Porsche and a Corvette. He tossed me the keys to the Corvette and he jumped into his Porsche, and we went into the desert and had fun racing around and making doughnuts in the dirt. He liked speed: I remember Andre zooming past me doing Mach 1. It was crazy.

Then we went to the casinos, where he threw some quarters into the slots. He won a $20 jackpot in quarters, and the next morning in church, he dropped all the quarters into the offering plate. I had a feeling that churches in Las Vegas were used to receiving "tithes and offerings" in that manner.

It was about this time that Andre started making a lot more than a handful of quarters. He signed a big racket endorsement deal for $4 million, but that was the tip of the proverbial iceberg. He probably made $25 million during his breakthrough year. Suddenly, overnight, Andre became a very rich young man, and it's very hard to maintain your focus on the Lord when you are surrounded by incredible wealth because money, and lots of it, buys influence and status in today's culture.

Another thing was happening at this heady time in the late 1980s. As Andre was reaping so much publicity—and writers were still employing the "born-again Christian" phrase with his name—he started getting letters. Letters from Christians telling him to get a haircut. That he looked like a girl. And get rid of the earring.

For the most part, they were terribly judgmental letters and mean-spirited to boot. Not at all loving. Phil would give me a bunch to read, and all I could do was shake my head.

Andre's response was to rebel, and the first manifestation of that was swearing on the court. If he didn't like a call or was losing, he rained f-bombs at the chair umpire, linesmen — himself. It was like he wanted to show the world: *See? I'm not @#$%-ing perfect!*

We had a falling out after I confronted Andre on a different issue that I will not discuss. Then I left the tour in 1992, the same year he won his first Grand Slam when he broke through at Wimbledon, beating Goran Ivanovic in five scintillating sets. I was truly happy for him.

Like millions of tennis fans everywhere, I watched from a distance as Andre reached the heights of tennis and experienced the lows during a long career, like when he fell to No. 141 in 1997. He had a great comeback when he completed a career Grand Slam by winning in Paris in 1999, and then he went on to have some of his best years ever in his early thirties.

I was saddened to read his acclaimed autobiography, *Open*, which was released in 2009. Saddened to read how Christians hurt him early on. Saddened to read what he said about other Christian players like Michael Chang. Saddened because he tiptoed around the topics that were eternal.

If I could sit across a table and break bread with Andre today, the first thing I'd say is, "Andre, when I first met you, you were like a little brother. I loved your enthusiasm, passion, determination, generosity, flamboyance, and your freedom to be *you*. You were the darling of the tennis world. You had made tennis fun to watch again!"

Then I'd continue: "As with all great players . . . superstars . . . that couldn't last—ask LeBron James—and people started to misinterpret your actions. They loved how you applauded by tapping your racquet with the palm of your left hand when your opponent made a great shot, but before long they called it arrogant. Really? The press started taking your friends' comments out of context and slamming you with their words, causing strife between friends. And then there were the haters . . . there always are.

"When you started talking about your faith, like after the Memphis championship in 1988, the expectations on you, on your behavior, and on your time began to mount, along with judgmental comments from people who had their *own* interest at heart. Not yours, not God's. It was *crazy!*

"So you retreated. Pushed them away. Cussed. Threw your racquet. Tanked a match. Showed them you weren't perfect . . . and weren't the 'savior' of tennis. Maybe then they would leave you alone. They clouded the reality of God's love for you and showed a perverted view of Christianity. I'd run from that, too!

"Now that I'm a dad with boys the age you were when we shared a slice of life together. My sons are spirited, talented, competitive and fun loving, but when they are pushed, they push back. I understand more clearly where you were coming from.

"People come into your life for a season. I was there for you for a couple of years, and then our paths diverged. I am thankful for the time I knew you and wish you continued blessing on your journey. May it lead you closer to the One who loves you most."

Two of the players I became closest with during my twelve years on the tour were Kenny Thorne (above) and Bryan Shelton (below). Separated by one month at birth, they grew up together in Alabama and were teammates at Georgia Tech.

9
MEN'S DRAW
Great Guys I Knew on the Tour

Two of the players I grew closest to on the tour were a couple of great guys you've probably never heard of or don't remember. I'm talking about Kenny Thorne and Bryan Shelton.

They became buddies in their preteens when they'd run into each other at junior tournaments in Alabama during the mid-1970s. Bryan was from Huntsville, Alabama, which was a small-city tennis hotbed during the boom years. His mother played some tennis and was involved with the Alabama Tennis Association. His father, a retired Army career officer who wrote manuals and trained personnel on the technical aspects of missiles, didn't play much at all.

"I first picked up a racket when I was eight years old," Bryan said. "I started playing local tournaments and found success rather early, so I thought I was pretty good at the age of ten. Then I entered a statewide tournament and lost to the number-one player in Alabama love-and-love. That's when I realized that maybe I wasn't so good and that I better start practicing. Tennis is an expensive sport, and a lot of players came from pretty wealthy families. My family was middle class, so there had to be sacrifices made for me to continue playing tennis."

As for Kenny, he grew up playing tennis in Arkansas until his family moved to Florence, Alabama, just before his freshman year of high school, because his father got a job with Reynolds Metals. The Thorne family was middle class as well, but the problem with Florence was that there wasn't *any* tennis happening. Kids were into football or hunting and fishing—not hitting a fuzzy optic yellow ball over the net. There wasn't a tennis court around for miles.

Despite the lack of opportunity, Kenny wanted to keep playing because he loved the game and had developed into a good junior player. The nearest opportunity to get coaching and practice with other juniors was in Huntsville, seventy miles to the east. His parents racked up the miles on U.S. Highway 72 so that Kenny could take lessons from Bill Tym, who was part of the founding leadership of the U.S. Professional Tennis Association (USPTA), a trade group of teaching pros around the country. (And a rival organization to Peter Burwash International, I might add.)

Bryan was also part of the after-school program with Coach Tym, who ran his program with military bearing and precision. He preached the gospel of thinking positively and expecting the best. He was big on making every minute count: if you were on the court, you were either practicing or playing with purpose. If you were off the court, you were reading a book or doing something constructive—not messing around or doing nothing.

"Bill was a solid, solid coach who we feared at first but as we grew up, we learned to respect him," Kenny explained. "I would drill with him every day after school, despite the long distance. It was a decent drive, and one day when I was fifteen years old, Coach Tym spoke with my parents about me coming to live with him and his wife, Wanda, so I didn't have to make the 140-mile round-trip drive each day. They agreed, and for two years, I lived in Huntsville."

As part of Coach Tym's junior program, Kenny and Bryan became inseparable, hitting for hours under the hot Alabama sun and playing doubles together in regional and national tournaments. "Kenny and I were able to push each other to be better players," Bryan said. "I'm a month older, so I always told Kenny that I was a month wiser on the court."

The friendship continued into college, where they arrived as a package deal on the campus of Georgia Tech in Atlanta, battling each other for positions on the team and battling against other teams for wins. They both became All-Americans and were ranked among the top college players in the country, which gave them the desire to continue playing tennis after graduation.

When their senior years at Georgia Tech were in the books, they decided to strike out on the professional tour — together. Remember the story about how I arranged housing for a couple of American players in Germany through Sportler-ruft-Sportler? That was for Kenny and Bryan during their first trip to Europe.

Kenny remembers his "welcome to pro tennis" moment. Back in 1989, during his rookie season, he was trolling for ATP points in future events and not making much headway. He also tried to qualify at some of the main draw events, where sixty-four entrants were trying to claw their way into the tournament. Only four players would make it. (Eight players can qualify for Grand Slam events).

At the tour stop in Los Angeles, held every summer on the campus of UCLA, Kenny caught fire and played his way into the main draw. Waiting for him in the first round was Peter Lundgren, a Swedish player who would go on to coach Roger Federer early in his great career. Lundgren was ranked fortieth in the world at the time, but Kenny's hot hand continued and he won a great match.

Kenny went to the posted draw to see whom he would play in the second match. He followed his name, looked at the bracket below him . . . and saw that he would play the winner of a match between Michael Chang and some guy named Pete Sampras.

Everyone had heard of Michael Chang because of what happened three months earlier when Michael had captured the French Open at the age of seventeen, becoming the youngest male to win a Grand Slam. Now Michael was playing his first tournament in Southern California, where he had honed his game in the San Diego area before moving to Placentia, an Orange County suburb not far from Disneyland.

Pete Sampras was from the Los Angeles area, too, but he hadn't had much success since turning pro a year earlier. He was eighteen years old, and while those in the know thought he was destined for greatness, the lanky Sampras was struggling to get past the first round in main-draw tournaments.

Michael and Pete were kind of like the Kenny and Bryan of Southern California junior tennis — playing and practicing against each other since they were elementary school kids. A month before Michael's breakthrough win at the French, he and Pete had trained on clay in nearby Palm Desert with José Higueras, a former tour player from Spain. And in the irony of ironies, they had flown to Paris to play Roland Garros, where they had traveled 6,000 miles to play each other in the first round.

Michael won that match on clay, 6-1, 6-1, 6-1, and would go on to win the tournament, of course. Now the luck of the draw had them playing each other again in Los Angeles, just three months later, and Michael continued his mastery of Pete. (This would change very shortly.)

So Kenny would face Michael in the second round, a night match when Hollywood celebrities came out to see top-flight tennis. "I remember walking out for my match and seeing Johnny Carson, the late-night host of the *Tonight Show*, in the first row behind the baseline," Kenny said. "I was terrified. I had to even concentrate on how to walk out and sit down because I was so nervous. Well, forty-eight minutes later, we were done. Michael beat me very quickly, 6-1, 6-1.

"We carried our bags back to the locker room, and I sat down on a bench and held my head in my hands. I wasn't disconsolate, but it was apparent that there was a huge gap between me and a player of Michael's caliber. Then I felt a pat on the shoulder. It was Michael. 'It's okay, Kenny,' he said. 'You just need a little more experience out there. It'll come.'

"I looked up. Michael was just a kid—someone who should have been getting ready for his senior year of high school. I was a twenty-three-year-old college graduate, and here's this kid telling me not worry—I just needed more experience. I know he meant well, and I was happy to take his advice, but it sure was a rude awakening."

Kenny never had it easy out there. I don't know how many times he lost in the last round of the qualies, but there were too many heartbreaking moments, like the time I saw him lose a final-set tiebreaker in a match that would have allowed him to play in the U.S. Open.

But in his own way, Kenny was the King of the Qualies. One season, he qualified nine straight times in the dog-eat-dog competition. "I had a tour representative come up to me and tell me that I had set a record, qualifying so many times consecutively. And I was like, *Oh, great.* It wasn't easy, winning three matches to get into the main draw. The level is pretty high, but playing those qualifying events gave me a lot of match experience. It's too bad that I couldn't win more matches once I got into the main draw."

Bryan took his lumps as well in his early years on the tour. During his rookie season, he had played the qualies in Key Biscayne and lost in the second round. He decided to stick around the tournament for a few days and get in some good practice. He liked hanging out in the player's lounge because it was cool to watch all the big players march through.

One afternoon, the lady at the front desk put the phone on her shoulder and shouted, "Anyone want to hit with Ivan Lendl?" This was when Lendl was winning Grand Slams and had planted himself as the No. 1 player in the world.

Bryan nearly jumped out of his chair. "I'll hit with Ivan!" he cried out, and the next he knew, he was driving over to a nearby hotel to meet the Czech and his coach, Tony Roche, a great Australian player from the 1960s.

"I introduced myself, and then we started practicing," Bryan said. "I was extremely nervous to be hitting balls with the best player in the world. After we were good and warmed up, Ivan announced that we were going to play these various rally games, and every time you lost a game, you had to drop down and do twenty push-ups.

"For two hours, I lost every game I played, and Ivan

seemed to enjoy watching me do push-ups as punishment. I was exhausted, and then we played a final rally game. I somehow came to game point for me, and I took a short ball and approached hard on his backhand. He ran and ripped the ball up the line but missed by an inch. I had finally won a game!

"Ivan immediately dropped down and did his twenty push-ups. When he was done, he looked me directly in the eye and said, 'In the finals, I will make that shot ten out of ten times.' He was right. Ivan went on to win the Key Biscayne tournament that year because of the confidence he had. I saw that he was one of the hardest workers out there, and I can assure you that I slept very well after practicing with him. Ivan helped me understand what it takes to succeed in pro tennis. We developed a friendship, and I practiced with him many times after that."

Working hard with Lendl raised the level of Bryan's game. By the 1989 U.S. Open, his rookie season, Bryan's ranking was high enough to play in Flushing Meadow, where he got to play Jimmy Connors in the second round. This was a night match at Louis Armstrong Stadium before 18,000 rabid fans—the biggest stage Bryan had ever played on.

Bryan walked onto the court, thinking about when he had been an eleven-year-old ball boy for Connors at a pro tournament in Birmingham, Alabama. Now, thirteen years later, he was playing one of his childhood idols before a packed house in New York. Bryan played loose and played great, taking the first set in a tiebreaker. Jimbo, then thirty-seven years old, drew upon his vast experience to take the next three sets, however, but Bryan learned he could play with the big boys. He even beat Andre Agassi, 6-4, 6-4, at the Lipton

International at Key Biscayne in 1992.

He had his greatest success on grass, where he became the first African-American to win a singles title since Arthur Ashe when he captured the Hall of Fame Championships on the greensward of Newport, Rhode Island in the summer of 1991. He defended his Newport title in 1992—the only two tournament wins in his career—and raised his ranking to a career-high No. 55.

Bryan learned something about titles and rankings: you are never truly satisfied with what you have. "When you're 200 in the world, you want to get in the low 100s. And then when you reach No. 100, you want to get at least to No. 75. Even when I got to No. 55, I was trying to figure out a way to get a little higher," he said.

That's normal to want more—but Bryan knew that he needed to keep an eternal perspective out there on the court. His mindset became this: *I'm out here playing tennis because I want to glorify God.*

"I worked hard to glorify God because I didn't want tennis to be all about my ranking or me playing tennis before thousands of people or a nationwide audience in the millions," he said. "In a way, that took the pressure off."

That ideal was put to the test in 1994 when he lost *ten* first-round matches in a row and was ranked in the low hundreds, meaning that he was just outside the cutoff line for Wimbledon. Back to qualifying.

"In the first round of qualifying, I didn't play very well, but I won," he said. "I didn't play great in the second round, but I still advanced. But then in the last round, I played great and got into the main draw of Wimbledon. When I looked at my draw, I saw that I was playing Michael Stich of Germany in the first round. Michael had won Wimbledon in 1991 and was seeded second. Prior to the match, I had one of the best practices ever. The tennis ball looked as big as a basketball. When I walked out onto the court, I had a peace about me that I was going to be successful that day."

Here's how *Los Angeles Times* writer Gene Wojciechowski described what happened next:

"Stick another tombstone outside infamous Court No. 2, known as the 'graveyard of champions,' and busier than ever Wednesday as unseeded Bryan Shelton shocked the late great second-seeded Michael Stich in three 'did-you-see-that?' sets. The American's 6-3, 6-4, 6-4 victory so thoroughly exasperated Stich that the former Wimbledon champion stormed off the sun-soaked court and didn't bother to look back. Earlier, the games slipping by one by one, Stich had delivered a wonderful overhead smash to his equipment bag, followed soon thereafter by another tantrum that left a thin divot in the turf."

Stich was the first No. 2 seed to be knocked by a qualifier in sixty-three years. "Afterwards," Bryan said, "Michael talked to the media and said if I played this guy one hundred times, I would beat him ninety-nine times. But our match was that one day."

Bryan was more gracious in defeat because he had the right perspective after becoming a Christian late in his freshmen year at Georgia Tech. He had seen a godly example in his doubles partner, Kenny, who became a Christian through Young Life in high school, as well as his assistant coach at Georgia Tech, Gary Niebur. Then Mark Price, a point guard with the Cleveland Cavaliers, shared what it meant to have a relationship with Jesus Christ at an outreach event, and Bryan accepted Christ into his heart.

Bryan and Kenny were absolute regulars at my

Wednesday night Bible studies for the players; I could always count on them. They were full of great questions and shared a hunger to learn more about what God had to say in the Bible.

When Bryan qualified for the U.S. Open and played his second round match against Jimmy Connors on national television, I spoke to his parents before he took the court. They couldn't say enough about how pleased they were that my wife, Robin, and I were out on the tour.

"How thrilled we were when Bryan called and told us he had just been to a Bible study," his mother said. "As parents, we were concerned about sending our son onto a tour that was so worldy and self-oriented. We feared he would have no Christian fellowship. What a blessing to know you are there for guys like Bryan to support, encourage, and to help keep their focus on Christ."

And then our home church, The Chapel, received a note from Kenny's parents that read:

> *Thank you for sending Fritz and Robin to minister and spread the Word of Christ to professional tennis players. They have been a wonderful answer to our prayers for fellowship and discipleship for our son, Kenny, who is on the tour. Praise God for your evangelistic vision!*
>
> *Dave and Peggy Thorne*

Getting feedback from the families of players was golden and a real encouragement. When attending the players' matches, I could often pick up something that I could share with them later.

I'd sit in on Bryan's matches every chance I had, and I noticed that he would reach into his tennis bag during changeovers and pull out several note cards. Each contained a Bible verse or a devotional thought.

I enjoyed watching Kenny's matches, too, since he always seemed to be the underdog every time he walked out onto the court. Kenny didn't win as much as Bryan, and he reached his career-high No. 121 in 1993. He did win two ATP doubles titles in 1994, but he and Bryan didn't partner each other on the court, even though they were partners in Christ.

There's a great story about Kenny that I had forgotten until he reminded me of it. At a tournament in Atlanta in the early 1990s, the players were invited to hear Christian author Ron Blue speak. Author of *Master Your Money*, Blue was passionate about the importance of having financial goals and exercising stewardship of the resources God gives us.

Kenny had married Bridget by this time, and money was tight since there were some weeks when Kenny earned zilch on the court. He and Bridget had a running joke about their finances: if Kenny wasn't winning, then their nightly treat would be the cheapie Kroger brand Neapolitan ice cream. If Kenny was winning and still in the tournament, then they'd go whole hog and buy a pint of Häagen-Dazs Swiss Almond ice cream to share in bed and spoon to each other.

So keep that thought in mind as Kenny and Bridget walk into a hotel conference room to hear Ron Blue speak. They looked around to see who else was there, and lo and behold, Andre Agassi was in the house. This would have been in the early 1990s—Andre's big hair days.

Ron commenced to doing his thing, talking about spending money wisely, not going into credit card debt, having a rainy day fund, and the like. When he asked for questions, young Andre raised his hand.

In the most sincere voice, he asked a heartfelt question in

total seriousness: "I want to be a good steward of my money, so what airplane do you think I should buy?"

"Andre was absolutely serious," Kenny said. "He wasn't being arrogant. He wasn't trying to show up the other players in the room. This was his world. He asked the question because he wanted to make the best decision possible on a major purchase. Of course, a major purchase for him was a $20 million airplane, and a major decision for us was whether we should buy the Kroger or the Häagen-Dazs ice cream that night."

Unfortunately, the Thornes ate a lot of Kroger ice cream, but they had some great nights when they broke out the Häagen-Dazs, like when he defeated top players like Richard Krajicek, Wayne Ferreira, Mark Philippoussis, and Todd Martin. Eventually, all good things come to an end, and Kenny had to move on.

Turns out he was in the right place at the right time when he was hired as the assistant coach of the Georgia Tech men's tennis program in 1997. He was such a dynamic presence at his alma mater that within a year, he was named to the newly created position of Director of Tennis and became the ninth head coach in Tech's men's tennis history. He was tasked with turning the Yellow Jackets into national contenders, as well as oversight of the women's tennis program.

This is where Kenny and Bryan's story comes full circle. As Kenny was looking for someone to lead the women's tennis team, there was only one person the school should hire: Bryan Shelton.

"Kenny called me and said there's an opening for the head coach of the women's tennis team," Bryan said. "He said, 'Do me a favor and meet with me and the athletic director and hear what we have to say.' I was coaching for the

USTA at the time, but I could see that this was a wonderful opportunity."

Bryan became the Georgia Tech's women's coach in 2000 and lifted the program to national prominence as well as an NCAA championship in 2007. He was named Intercollegiate Tennis Association (ITA) Coach of the Year the same year. (And Kenny was named ITA Coach of the Year in 2011 for guiding the Yellow Jackets to the round of 16 in the NCAA team championships.)

Alas, nothing is forever. In June 2012, Bryan decided to take on a new challenge by becoming the men's tennis coach at the University of Florida.

"It is with mixed emotions that I left Georgia Tech, a place that had been home to me and my family for many years," Shelton said. "These were thirteen of the best years of my life, and I owe Georgia Tech an incredible amount. Kenny Thorne is my best friend, and it was very special to work alongside him."

And now Bryan and Kenny will be coaching *against* each other in the SEC conference.

That's something I'll want to watch as well.

Gary Niebur

I mentioned Gary Niebur while telling Kenny Thorne's and Bryan Shelton's story because he was instrumental in their lives when they were playing at Georgia Tech, where Gary was the assistant coach at the time.

Gary has a great story, too, growing up in Southern California as a contemporary of Stan Smith. His father was Catholic, and his mother was Jewish, but she didn't want to have anything to do with religion because her mother had converted to Christian Science and insisted that her husband

(Gary's grandfather) not see any doctor when he became sick and later died.

When Gary was growing up and fifteen years old, his mother contracted cancer. She died on his sixteenth birthday. On the way home from the hospital, Gary asked his father where his mother was, and he said he did not know. Mad at God, Gary took his frustrations out on the tennis court, where he regularly threw his racket and railed to the high heavens after dumping sitters into the net.

"I kept beating myself up, which only made me play worse," Gary said. "I couldn't figure things out. One night, I asked God to reveal Himself to me, and slowly but surely, He did. I started attending a youth group at a nearby church. My brother came to faith, but I was still holding out. I did, however, feel unconditional love from the people who knew God. They cared about me not because I was a tennis player but in spite of that.

"Then one evening, the youth pastor opened up his Bible to John 3 and showed me what it meant to have a new life in Christ and be born again by the Holy Spirit. I thought about what he said, and two weeks later, I went over to his house one night, and we got on our knees and I prayed to receive Christ into my heart. I learned that 2 Corinthians 5:17 says that if anyone is in Christ, then he is a new creation and the old has gone and the new has come. The greatest manifestation of Christ was on the tennis court. God really didn't care whether I won or lost a match but was more concerned about my character and transforming my heart. When I grasped that, my whole game changed. Christ freed me from all that anger. Instead of getting tight during matches, I enjoyed the competition. I had total freedom."

Gary went on to play college tennis at Chico State in

Northern California and thought about getting into coaching a college program, but several coaches told him he should try his hand on the professional tour for a couple of years and see what happens. He bounced around the Challenger circuit and didn't make much headway. The first year he tried to qualify at Wimbledon, Gary got in touch with me and asked if I could find him housing with a Christian family.

I set Gary up with a local pastor named Jonathan Fletcher. Then I invited him to go to a Cliff Richard concert, but Gary had never heard of the famous British pop artist. He decided to go out to dinner instead, and at the restaurant, he ran into a British player named Sue Barker, who asked him to sit down with her. Sue had just broken off a relationship with . . . Cliff Richard, and that's all she wanted to talk about that night. Gary lent an ear as she poured out her heart. (Today, Sue Barker conducts the on-court interviews of the winners and losers of the Wimbledon singles, men and women.)

The following night, the Billy Graham Crusade was in London, and I asked Gary to join me and several players for the event at Wembley Stadium. "Fritz, you got me a seat right on the stage that night, and I had a phenomenal experience," Gary said.

After three-and-a-half years of trying to crack the main draws of major tournaments, Gary gave up the ghost and turned to college coaching. He got a job as the assistant coach of Georgia Tech, just as two promising players from Alabama joined the team. "I discipled Brian and Kenny for a couple of years, and I introduced Kenny's wife to him," Gary said.

Here's where God's world even gets smaller. These days Gary works for Stan Smith and his company, Stan Smith Events, where he serves as the president and runs the day-today operations. With their Southern California background, love for tennis, and common zeal to serve the Lord, the two have paired up to form a formidable doubles team in the area of providing exclusive services to corporate clients.

At big sporting events around the world — tennis' Grand Slam events, golf's majors, and quadrennial competitions likes the Olympic Games and soccer's World Cup — major corporations are looking to use those events to develop quality relationships with their clients and customers. That's where Stan Smith Events steps in, organizing relationship-building experience from golf and tennis challenges to cooking experiences and skeet-shooting experiences. In other words, if you're a Coca-Cola or Frito-Lay executive and want to invite your best clients to Wimbledon or the British Open golf tournament for a fun four days, Stan Smith Events will take care of every detail, large and small.

These days, Gary and his wife, Teresa, live in the Atlanta area with their daughters Sarah Gail, Lily, and Sophia, and enjoy investing their time mentoring engaged and newly married couples. He's also fulfilled a dream to build a children's home. La Casa de mi Padre in El Salvador became a reality several years ago, a home where abandoned children receive help, hope, healing, and love to turn their lives around.

That's what I like about Gary — working in God's economy.

Brian Page

In the summer of 1988, Brian Page turned pro after earning All-ACC honors playing at Clemson University. Brian finished college ranked in the Top Ten in career double wins. He was a pretty good doubles player on the pro circuit too, teaming up with players like Bryan Shelton, Ville Jansson, and others.

During one particular tournament, after hearing from his roommate, Kent Kinnear, about what I was doing on the tour, Brian approached me with a problem he was having with prayer.

"My prayers seem to be bouncing off the ceiling," he told me. Brian had been raised Catholic and said the prayers he read from his prayer book seemed empty and rote.

"Do you know who you are talking to?" I asked.

"No," Brian replied as he gave it some thought.

I gave Brian a book about how to know Christ and encouraged him to start reading the Book of John in the Bible with this question in mind: *Who is Jesus?*

When I saw Brian again at the next tournament, he came up to me and said, "I am ready to begin my relationship with Christ."

We prayed right there, and Brian started his journey with Christ that very day.

Juan Rios

"Have you met Juan yet? He's a brand new believer . . . you need to meet him."

"Hey, Fritz, I don't know if anyone has told you, but there's a player who needs to meet you. He's only been a Christian four weeks and has so many questions. I've been trying to answer them, but he needs to talk to you. I'll introduce you when I see him."

And so I met Juan . . . inquisitive, unashamed of his new faith, and spiritually hungry. We talked a couple of hours, and then he had to catch a flight to Palm Springs where he was playing his next tournament.

"Listen, Juan," I said, "I have a good friend in Palm

Another player I spent a lot of time with was Brian Page (above). I also had the privilege of marrying Brian and Carla.

Springs, Tim Clark. He's a teaching pro and a strong Christian. If you have any trouble or need anything, here's his number. Give him a call." Little did I know how God would use that simple statement to impact this young believer's life.

When Juan arrived in Palm Springs, his housing fell through. Tim was on his way to a Bible study when Juan called. Tim picked him up, took him to the Bible study, and made arrangements for Juan to stay with a Christian family who lived within walking distance of the tournament.

Juan had never attended a Bible study and wasn't quite sure what to expect. He couldn't believe how exciting it was to study God's Word in a group and learn what a passage really meant.

Juan had such a great time with the family that housed him that he stayed an extra week, studying the Bible and asking questions. It was exciting to see how God used the Body of Christ to nurture one of His children.

One day Juan called me from Puerto Rico full of excitement. He spent time with contacts I was able to find for him in the Caribbean Islands while playing tournaments there and was encouraged in his faith as he traveled. The most exciting thing was the reaction of his parents to his decision to follow Christ. They were ecstatic. His mother had been praying for him since he was a boy.

Ville Jansson

Finally, there's one other player I want to mention, and that's Ville Jansson, a Swedish player who came over to the U.S. to play at Northeast Louisiana State University in Monroe, Louisiana, earning All-America honors in 1986 while battling mononucleosis.

Each year, tennis players and their spouses gathered for the Pro Athletes Outreach conference. From the left: Kent Kinnear, Juan Rios, Norm Evans (a former Miami Dolphin player and president of PAO), Jimmy and Gina Arias, Doug Flack, Sandra and Ken Flack, and Robin and me.

Ville tried his hand on the Challenger circuit after he graduated, playing in small tournaments. His ranking never got higher than No. 243 in the world, but that didn't matter because it's stories like his that made all my years out on the tour so richly rewarding.

In fact, after I spoke with Ville—who's currently the Director of Tennis at the impressive Galleria Tennis Club in Houston—he sent me the nicest email, which I'll reprint here:

A message from Ville Jansson:
I was a player just out of college from Sweden. My faith was one where I knew of a Supreme Being and subscribed to the theory of intelligent design. I was content to not dwell any deeper, thinking the more I knew, the more I would miss out on life. I could not have been any more wrong.

Through my travels on the tennis circuit, God connected me with Fritz Glaus, Kenny Thorne, Bryan Shelton, and another player, Kent Kinnear. They, along with my wife, Tonya, kept challenging me to read the Bible. I spent many hours firing questions at Fritz, which he patiently answered. He also suggested reading material to study.

In September 1989, Fritz suggested that I read Mere Christianity *by C.S. Lewis. I did, and it all started to come together for me. I now know that it was the prayers of my wife and friends that brought me to that point. I accepted Jesus as my Lord and Savior at a hotel room in Vancouver, British Columbia, that fall.*

I have stated many times that my playing career on the ATP tour was nothing special if you look at the prize money and titles. God, however, used my professional career for something more important. I received everlasting life, and no money or titles can ever measure up to that.

Ville's heartfelt message kind of says it all, doesn't it?

Nothing better than sitting down after a long day of tennis and ordering in pizza. From the left: Brian Page, Kenny Thorne, Nduka Odizor, myself, and Ville Jansson.

One happy group: Hank Pfister, Wendy White, Jenny Geddes, myself, Buzz Strode, and Bud Cox.

10
MIXED DOUBLES
Ladies of the Court

As you know, I followed the men's tour, but there were at least five tournaments a year where the men and women played at the same site during the 1980s. I'm speaking about the four Grand Slam tournaments (the French Open, Wimbledon, U.S. Open, and the Australian Open) plus the Lipton tournament in Key Biscayne, Florida.

The quartet of Grand Slam tournaments were my favorites because the players *knew* they were playing for more than silver chalices and the biggest purses in tennis—they were playing for history. Win a Grand Slam, and your tennis résumé was complete and doors opened around the world. Lifting a Grand Slam trophy above your head was also worth millions of dollars of endorsements.

I looked forward to the Big Four for reasons beyond temporal. This was my chance to plan ministry events and outreaches with the men *and* women players. I would line up interesting speakers or do chapel events like we did in London during Wimbledon. Many years, I coordinated these outreach happenings with my counterpart on the women's tour, Jenny Geddes, who traveled as a chaplain for a half-dozen years during the mid-1980s. We worked together to make the Grand Slam fortnights something special, which also gave me the opportunity to befriend some wonderful Christians on the women's tour. In this chapter, I'll introduce three of them, and they, too, have remarkable stories to tell.

Ros Fairbank-Nideffer

I first met Ros—short for Rosalyn—at the 1984 U.S. Open when Jenny Geddes introduced me to her. Ros was twenty-four at the time and already a Grand Slam winner in doubles, having captured the French Open twice. She was a solid Top 20 player in singles.

Ros enjoyed her greatest success on the slow red clay of Roland Garros even though she came from South Africa, where she grew up on hard courts and grass courts. She was a good doubles player because she was a great serve-and-volleyer with a solid overhead. She loved being at the net.

At Wimbledon that year, I spoke at one of the coed Bible studies and mentioned that I was going to Israel when the fortnight was over. "Would anyone like to join me?" I asked. "Going to the Holy Land would be an awesome experience."

Only one person was interested in making the trip—Ros Fairbank.

I gulped. We were both single, and when I explained that she was the only one who wanted to join me, I told her that I would totally understand if she wanted to back out.

"No, I'd still like to go," Ros said.

I know it sounds a little weird, but we traveled together to Tel Aviv and then on to Jerusalem. We stayed in separate hotel rooms, of course, and besides, there wasn't a spark of romance between us. She was a sister in Christ who had become a Christian a year earlier, and Ros said she wanted to experience the ancient land where Jesus walked and the Apostles started the Church. Everywhere you turn in Israel, you're experiencing biblical history with every step.

We based ourselves in Jerusalem, where I escorted Ros to all the top spots, like the tomb where Jesus supposedly lay following his death, the place of His crucifixion, the Wailing Wall, and the town of Bethlehem, which was just a few miles from Jerusalem. We also took day trips to the Dead Sea, Megiddo, and Capernaum on the Sea of Galilee with guides.

I asked Ros what she remembered most about our impressionable ten days in Israel, and she had several memories. "You were so outgoing and personable with everyone and wanted us to get to know the people," she recalled. "We certainly did some things that normal tourists don't get to do. I remember meeting some Arabs in Jerusalem, and they showed us how to smoke one of their pipes. They also invited us to sit down and share of cup of their very strong, bitter coffee. Another time, we were invited to someone's home, which was fascinating. I asked if I could use the bathroom, and when I went in, the toilet was a hole in the floor. That showed me right there how different we live."

Ros had another memory that wasn't so pleasant. It seems that I ate an apple without washing it and got really sick the next day—and then she got sick.

We felt totally safe in Israel and didn't have any incidents, but there was another time that Ros looked down the barrel of a gun and wondered if it was her time to meet the Lord. That incident happened when she was playing in New Orleans. She arrived in the Crescent City with her husband-to-be, Bob Nideffer, a couple of days before the start of the tournament. They were staying in a suite hotel, and one day, the two of them got into a tiff about how Ros had played a *practice* match. "Bob asked me to come to his room, and we got into a big argument. It took us an hour to work our way through things, and then he said, 'Let's go get some dinner.'

"We were hungry enough to skip returning back to my room to retrieve my wallet and purse. We walked to a restaurant a few blocks away from the hotel, had a nice meal, and then started strolling back on streets that weren't exactly in the nicest part of town. Suddenly, two teenage kids jumped out and blocked our path. One reached into his pocket and pulled out a gun, which he waved at me. 'Grab her bracelet!' he yelled at his friend, which he did.

"Then he pointed the gun at Bob's head. I got a very good look at the gun and wondered if I should grab it. Then the assailant barked, 'Give me your wallet!' Bob didn't have to be asked twice. After he handed his billfold over, the ringleader told us turn around and run, which we were grateful to do. So we took off, but as we looked back, we saw them running in the other direction. It was a scary situation, and I was fortunate that I didn't have my wallet and purse with me."

Born in 1960, Ros grew up in Durban, South Africa, the youngest of four children at a time when apartheid—a system of racial segregation—was the law of the land. She became a very good junior player and started traveling to international tournaments when she was seventeen. During her senior year of high school, she applied to the University of Texas and was offered a tennis scholarship. Her father, conservative and strict, balked at his daughter going to college so far from home. She told her family doctor that she really wanted to play tennis, and he convinced her father to let her go out on the professional tour for one year. "So I really have to thank my family doctor for my tennis career," she said.

Ros played a long time on the tour—twenty years—and was a bit of a late bloomer, reaching a career-high No. 15 in the world in 1990 when she was thirty years old. She was one of the last serve-and-and volleyers on the women's side, even coming in behind her second serve on grass and fast indoor surfaces. She wasn't afraid to charge the net on the clay of Roland Garros, where she got to the fourth round several times.

Just as there were only a handful of serve-and-volleyers in women's tennis, there were only a handful of Christian players on the women's tour. When I asked Ros why, she had a thoughtful answer. "When I was on the tour, I was so highly competitive that it was hard for me to be a Christian. I once asked Stan Smith how he reconciled being a believer and competing so hard, and he said you should go out there and play for the glory of God. That was a difficult concept for me to grasp because I was so hung up on winning. In fact, I still struggle with being competitive and being a Christian," she said.

Ros still plays the occasional age-group tennis tournament today. She is one of the top women players in the world in the senior women's 50s age group, and she won the International Tennis Federation Senior World Championships in her hometown of San Diego in 2012.

"Did you think the right way to play was to grit your teeth and hustle for the ball?" I asked. "Did you think you'd lose your edge if you didn't try so hard instead of trusting the Lord for the outcome?"

"I was too hung up on wanting to win instead of playing to the best of my ability," she replied. "So my worldly way of thinking was getting in the way, which was too bad because I know I could have been a better player. I say that because I can look back to a number of times when I would choke after getting ahead in a match. One time I was playing Martina Navratilova in the quarterfinals of Wimbledon on what was really my best surface, grass. I had her down a set with a point to go ahead 5-2. But I tightened up and made some careless mistakes because it was so important for me to win. I wanted to win for me rather than for the glory of God."

Ros said even when she played in the "old ladies" doubles at Wimbledon—the senior events in her thirties and forties—she still could not give up that intense desire to win. Old habits die hard. But she did learn a different lesson on the tour that stuck with her.

"I was playing the Virginia Slims of Richmond back in 1983," she began, referring to a tour stop in Richmond, Virginia. "I was newly converted to Christ. One of the tough questions I was wrestling with was whether God expected me to tithe 10 percent of my prize money to Him. I talked to other Christians on the tour, and they told me it was best to take it to God in prayer. So a week before Richmond, I told the Lord if you want me to tithe, give me a sign by having me win the tournament. Now, the chances of me winning that tournament were slim and none. Martina Navratilova was in the field, and she was seeded No. 1.

"And wouldn't you know it . . . I won the singles *and* the doubles, and it was my only significant singles victory as a professional during my two decades on the tour. You better believe that I started tithing after that, and I can remember sponsoring about six kids from Save the Children. God really taught me a lesson that week about how to honor Him with everything I have."

Now that's what I call a percentage play . . .

Wendy White

Wendy White, like Ros Fairbank, was born in 1960 and was also raised in a Christian home while growing up in the suburbs of Atlanta. When she was around fifteen and competing in national tournaments, her mom would give her books to help her grow in her faith in Christ.

"I was really seeking to know the Lord personally," she said. "When I was playing these out-of-state tournaments in the juniors, I was going up against very good players and realized that I needed God's help. I reached out to the Lord and sought Him more than I ever had, but this was the start of a two-year process. You see, I was asking God to help me, but only in certain areas—like my tennis. I had a lot to learn about Him," she said.

Wendy was attending a Christian high school at the time, which included classes in the New Testament and Old Testament. Her New Testament teacher made the class memorize many Bible verses, including Ephesians 2:8-9, which says, "For it is by grace you have been saved, through faith—and this is not from yourselves, it is the gift of God—not by works, so that no one can boast."

Having an athletic background, Wendy had a works-based "performance" mindset when it came to Christianity. "I had always believed in God, and I thought I was a Christian because of the things I did—going to church, attending a youth group, and going to a Christian school. Then I began to understand that Christianity was not about a religious effort, or doing something for God, or trying to earn His acceptance, but it was about having a relationship with God through Jesus Christ. I needed to believe and receive God's gift of His Son into my heart."

After graduating from high school and enrolling at Rollins College in Winter Park, Florida, Wendy was attending a Bible study at a local church, where the leader of the study challenged her. "Have you ever accepted Jesus as your Lord and Savior and been assured of your salvation?" asked the Bible study leader.

Those words convicted Wendy. She needed that relationship with God, and that's when she decided to publicly pray to receive Jesus Christ as her Lord and Savior. "The difference I felt after doing that was a peace in knowing that Christ was inside my heart, changing me from the inside out, just as He said in Philippians 2:13: 'For it is God who is at work in you to will and to act according to his good purpose.' "

From now on, her motivation to do well in tennis was no longer just personal ambition but an effort to give it her all, as unto the Lord, in whatever she did on the court and to give Him the glory. "Becoming a Christian also helped me in having a much broader and eternal perspective on tennis and life," she said. "No longer was I weighed down by the ups and downs of winning and losing matches and worrying about my ranking."

Wendy had started playing tennis at the age of eight—at a horseback riding camp of all places. Like many young girls, she was fascinated by horses and riding them, but at this particular summer horseback camp, tennis was part of the daily program. She was introduced to the game and loved it. Something about hitting a ball with a racket appealed to her, and when she got home, she told her parents that she didn't want to ride horses anymore. She wanted to play tennis.

Atlanta is a hotbed for the game of a lifetime, and she quickly rose through the ranks to become a nationally

Wendy White was seventeen years old when she and eighteen-year-old Kathy Jordan blazed a trail to the quarterfinals of the 1978 U.S. Open women's doubles event. Wendy went on to have a fine professional career, reaching a career-high No. 21.

ranked player in the juniors, winning or being a finalist in more than thirty national championships. Her stellar junior career earned her a tennis scholarship to Rollins College in Winter Park, Florida. During her freshman year, Wendy did something smart—she got plugged into the Fellowship of Christian Athletes (FCA), which was a big help to her. Cindy Sain Neely, an FCA assistant director, helped Wendy grow in her faith.

Like Ros Fairbank-Nideffer, Wendy struggled with how to view herself as a Christian while playing tournament matches. Could she compete with a killer instinct, take-no-prisoners attitude on the court and still be a Christian?

"Cindy told us that there was no doubt about it—we could be Christians and still compete out there. When I understood that Christ gave His all for me, I wanted to give my all for Him. That made me work harder on the tennis court. I did not want to win for someone's approval. I wanted to win for the Lord, and in Christ, I had a better and stronger motivation. Some people want to play out of their anger or for themselves or for the money, but I believe all those motivations limit you. What helped me was having a different perspective not normally found in the tennis world."

She had just graduated from high school when she played the first U.S. Open held at Flushing Meadow in 1978. She was seventeen years old, and in the doubles, she teamed up with eighteen-year-old junior Kathy Jordan. Together the pair of high schoolers blazed a trail to the quarterfinals.

"Kathy and I were just little punks, and in our quarterfinal match, we would be playing against Virginia Wade and Françoise Durr. Virginia had won Wimbledon the year before and was one of the best players in the world, so this was a tremendously exciting match for us. Kathy and I were staying with the Junior Federation Cup team in Manhattan, and on the morning of the match, we took a boat tour around the island of Manhattan. When we got back, we learned that our match had been moved up and we had to get out to Flushing Meadow in a hurry. Shortly after we arrived, we were rushed out on court and lost in three sets, but it was quite a match. That was my fondest memory of playing doubles at the U.S. Open."

Wendy continued to play professional tournaments — as an amateur — during her first two years of college, obtaining a world ranking of No. 65 by the end of her sophomore year. Although Wendy gained invaluable experience through collegiate tennis and enjoyed the camaraderie of playing for a team, her ultimate goal was to turn pro as well as to graduate from Rollins with a degree in Business Communications.

Being faced with a critical decision of when to turn pro, Wendy found comfort and strength through Psalm 37:4-5: "Delight yourself in the Lord, and he will give you the desires of your heart; commit your way to the Lord; trust also in him and he will do this."

Wendy ended her collegiate tennis career her sophomore year with the AIAW National Championship singles title and an important life lesson that would help her throughout her professional tennis career. She learned that if she trusted God with every area of her life, He would take care of her.

Within a year after Wendy turned pro, she had significant wins over players in the Top 10 in the world, including Billie Jean King, Virginia Ruzici, Wendy Turnbull, and others, which helped lift her ranking to No. 21 in the world. She continued to attend Rollins College her junior and senior years, graduating on time while competing on the women's professional tennis circuit.

She was happy when Jenny Geddes started traveling as a tour chaplain in the early 1980s. "I had met Jenny when she was an assistant coach at UCLA, and Jenny had already cultivated some good relationships with college players who were going out on the professional tour. It helped that during the early 1980s there were a lot of American college players on the professional tour. Jenny led Bible studies during the week and then would go out to dinner with us. She was a good listener and let the players share what was on their hearts. She was always asking questions or asking if you needed help to study a certain part of Scripture."

Carol Fullerton, who played collegiate tennis and competed on the women's pro satellite circuit for a short season, also spent several years on the women's pro circuit in a similar capacity as Jenny Geddes, ministering to the players and helping to lead Bible studies. The gatherings were not huge, but there were always four or five players that got together like Ros Fairbank, Cami Benjamin, Betsy Nagelsen, Gretchen Magers, and Lucy Gordon. "At the Grand Slams, the fellowships were a lot bigger when you, Fritz, brought in a lot of the guys," Wendy said.

At Wimbledon, I helped organize a radio interview on a Christian station for Wendy with Margaret Court, the great Australian champion of the 1960s who won all four Grand Slam tournaments in 1970 (the first women to do that in the Open era) and twenty-four Grand Slam singles championships.

"I was just out of college, so you can imagine how impressed I was with Margaret Court because all that she had done in tennis," Wendy said. "This happened during one of those years that past champions were honored at

Wimbledon, and Margaret said that if she had known then what she knows now about Christ, she would've been a better player. In my mind, she had done everything you could ever do in tennis. I was so impressed with her humility and her strength in the Lord. It was a real special moment for me to be around Margaret Court."

Wendy, who stayed inside the Top 50 for eight consecutive years during her twenties, remembers the time when she was playing an indoor tournament in Chicago, and Martina Navratilova was on the court. She broke a string, and a tour official asked if anyone could go into the locker room and grab another racket out of Martina's tennis bag. Since Wendy was nearby, she scooted into the locker room and found Martina's travel bag. She was about to reach for a racket when a Chihuahua named K.D. (for Killer Dog) peeked out of the bag and started barking like crazy.

"Martina would take her dog with her to all the tournaments, and even though she was a tiny dog, her bark sounded like a Rottweiler," Wendy laughed. "I had forgotten that Martina took her super killer dog everywhere. I did not want to get near that bag, nor did any of the other players in the locker room. We cracked up about it, but Martina had to come back to the locker room to get another racket for herself."

When Wendy was on tour, she often got confused with two players with the same last name—Anne White and Robin White—especially Anne White, who created quite a sensation at Wimbledon in 1985. It seems that she was warming up for her match on an outer court against Pam Shriver when she took off her tracksuit to reveal an . . . alabaster, one-piece Lycra body stocking that was, well, skintight from her plunging neckline to her twinkling toes. The crowd tittered and it wasn't long before all the male photographers rushed to Anne's court to take scandalous photo after scandalous photo of the form-fitting outfit.

The British tabloids had a field day, of course, and Wendy says people ask her to this day if she was the one who wore the white bodysuit.

Wendy had a fine pro career, staying inside the Top 50 for eight consecutive years during her twenties. She is also one of the few moms to play professional tennis when she married Scott Prausa in 1990 and gave birth a year later to Courtney. She returned to the circuit, but something must have been in the water because she quickly became pregnant again. With the arrival of Kelsey in 1993, Wendy retired to start a new season—busy mom. Cassie was born in 1997, and Matthew came along in 1999.

Wendy has kept a hand in tennis by coaching as an independent pro in the North Atlanta area as well as helping with FCA camps and sport outreaches. She teaches PE/Health classes and coaches the high school tennis team at Horizon Christian Academy, where her kids attend school.

In our interview, she said some very nice things. "Fritz, you meant so much to us out there," she began. "You challenged us and encouraged us and motivated us to stand strong in our faith. You watched our matches, and if you and Jenny had not stepped out in complete faith, then there would not have been the spiritual continuity among the tennis players. It is to easy on the tennis circuit to do your own thing and go your own way. Fritz, you really made a difference for the believers and non-believers, too. I just want to tell you how much we appreciated having you there."

Thanks, Wendy. That's very kind of you to say.

Lucy Gordon

Lucy Gordon grew up as the daughter of Alex Gordon, a well-known teaching professional who taught at the Hotel del Coronado across the bay from downtown San Diego. You'd think that her father would have put a sawed-off racket in her left hand when she was a toddler, but Lucy didn't play much tennis in her early years because she was involved in too many school activities. She did play on her high school team, but her father never pushed her to play seriously.

Thanks to her father's contacts, however, she got a partial scholarship to play at the University of San Diego, even though she had no record in junior tennis. Lucy also wanted to stay close to home because her father was battling terminal cancer as she entered USD. She played No. 5 on the team, but after her father tragically died, she threw herself into tennis as a way to cope with her grief. Lucy rose to No. 1 the following year and had a very good season.

Lucy decided to transfer to UCLA, where she could compete at the highest levels of college tennis. Jenny Geddes was the assistant coach at the time. Lucy wasn't a Christian when she played at UCLA, and in fact, she and her teammate and doubles partner, Kathy O'Brien, made a promise to each other on a plane flight home from the NCAA Championships. Their vow: never to become Christians.

The reason Lucy felt that way was because she was fighting God, who had surrounded her with Christian influences like Jenny Geddes and teammate Karin Huebner. Their sunny dispositions and loving manner permeated their beings. *The fragrance of Christ.*

"Looking back, I can see where I was on a path to actually finding God, and two months later, I broke my vow and became a Christian," Lucy said. "Nine months later, Kathy

Lucy Gordon was a late bloomer, making it to the pros despite not playing much junior tennis while growing up in San Diego.

committed her life to Christ as well. I had a lot of pain in my life growing up, and I think God just won me through Karin Huebner's love and the leading of the Holy Spirit."

When she graduated from UCLA, Lucy—being footloose and fancy free—decided to see the world and play some professional tennis. While on the road, she often roomed with Wendy White and spent a lot of time with Jenny Geddes, who had left UCLA to join me in tennis ministry.

It would be great to say that after Lucy became a Christian and turned pro that her game suddenly jumped several levels or that she started beating players who had been dusting her. That didn't happen. Lucy didn't become a world-beater or enjoy the kind of results that Ros and Wendy did, but she still had some great life experiences.

Lucy was on the tour for three-and-a-half years before getting into college coaching at Trinity University. "It was quite lonely, competitive and cutthroat out there on the tour," she said. "I didn't like how your whole value was found in your ranking. I had a hard time with that because I didn't value people according to where they stood in the world rankings."

Lucy was part of a group who joined me on a missions trip to Korea, China, and Hong Kong in 1988 before the Olympic Summer Games in Seoul that year. We played with some of their top juniors and gave tennis clinics, but our main purpose was to share Jesus' love and our faith in countries that rarely heard about the Gospel. Of course, we had to be very careful what we did and said in China, where we were monitored around the clock. Back then in those pre-Tiananmen Square days, China was much more closed than it is today.

One time when we sat down for dinner with some of our

Chinese hosts, we all received a plate of strange-looking food. I looked closely, and then a light went on: I was being served pickled duck foot! Webbing and all!

Lucy wasn't about to eat it, but I knew it would have been rude to refuse this delicacy, so I made of show of picking up the webfoot with my chopsticks and plopping it into my mouth. Yum-yum, I pantomimed to my hosts.

Lucy, along with Cami Benjamin, did their best not to crack up.

All in a day's work, I figured.

Cami Benjamin

Like Hank Pfister, Cami Benjamin grew up playing on the sun-baked courts of Bakersfield in Central California. Her father, Carl, who played college tennis at Central State College in Xenia, Ohio, 175 miles from my hometown of Brewster, introduced her to the game.

Carl Benjamin wasn't a teaching pro like Hank Sr., but he definitely had his own ideas about playing the game. A math professor at Bakersfield College who liked using angles on the court, Carl would feed Cami bucket after bucket of balls when his classroom work was over, starting when Cami was six years old. Cami became one of those unorthodox lefties, full of crafty spins and crazy angles.

You could see that Camille—her given name—was a smart player the way she utilized the entire court. She was also a trailblazer, in a manner of speaking, in the way she hit with heavy topspin and for being an African-American in what was pretty much a lily-white sport before the 1980s.

The generations of players before Cami hit the ball much flatter without much spin. Cami, on the other hand, was taught by her father to impart lots of topspin. Carl refused to

Cami Benjamin was an unorthodox lefty whose game was full of crafty spins and crazy angles. She could also hit the ball a ton, which is why friends called her "Cami Whammy."

change her strokes or the way she sometimes swung at high volleys, which, before the 1990s, was rarely done. Today, of course, lots of players will take high balls out of the air and hit a swinging volley, but Cami was one of the first. Friends gave her a nickname: Cami Whammy.

By her early teens, she was one of the best juniors in the country and was the No. 1-ranked junior in the 16-and-under age group in 1981, when she was fifteen years old. Several USTA coaches wanted to work with her, but they mentioned wanting to change her grip, her strokes, and many other parts of her game, believing that her noodle-arm, bent-wrist topspin stroke was too unorthodox. Cami and her father squashed those attempts quickly, however. They wanted to do things their way and not take the traditional route.

Cami turned pro at age 16 and rose quickly out of the satellite tournaments and into main-draw events. She was beating name players like Helena Sukova, Andrea Temesvari, Ros Fairbank, and another African-American player on the rise, Zina Garrison. But when Cami came out of nowhere to reach the semifinals of the 1984 French Open at the age of seventeen, the tennis world took notice.

Playing with a halo of Afro hair and white-rimmed over-sized glasses, the gangly Cami strode onto Court Central that June afternoon trailing one of the legends of the game: Chris Evert. She started the first game against Chris's serve strongly, jerking her well-known opponent around the court. On break point, a severely angled cross-court backhand just missed the line—and it was like Cinderella's carriage turned into a pumpkin. Chris held, broke Cami, and then the floodgates burst open. Less than an hour later, Cami had been double-bagled, 6-0, 6-0. The light rain hitting her glasses during the match didn't help her cause.

Even though a measure of hype was poured on Cami for reaching the semifinals of a Grand Slam tournament, she discovered that all the attention and adulation evaporated nearly as quickly as it took to shake hands with Chris Evert. The yo-yoing of fame made her question what she was doing out there on the tennis tour. What was the significance of traveling around the world and hitting a little yellow tennis ball across the net? At times, that seemed so inane.

As the early-round losses piled up following her Roland Garros breakthrough, life felt empty to her. The unexpected loss of her grandfather shortly after the 1984 French Open added to the identity crisis she was going through.

Following her grandfather's death, Cami was in Indianapolis, Indiana, for a tournament. Back in the day, players didn't make nearly the princely sums they earn today, and many lower-ranked players accepted "housing" from local families who volunteered to open up their home to the players.

"I was traveling with my friend Vicki Nelson, and she lost early," Cami remembers. "I was going through all this turmoil and felt like I needed a friend. I asked Vicki to stay, but she wanted to go home. I protested, but it did no good. Then the lady of the house gave me a book by Christian author Tim LaHaye called *Spirit-Controlled Temperament*, which was about the basic human temperaments and how God can use them. I wasn't much of a reader back then, so I tossed the book in my suitcase."

A few weeks later, she was playing a tournament in Florida and was watching Vicki Nelson play a match. Suddenly, Vicki asked Cami if she could run to the locker room and get her a hat. Moving quickly through the bleachers, Cami bumped her knee and cut it open, resulting in ten stitches.

She suddenly had a lot of down time. Bored with her leg in a splint, Cami picked up *Spirit-Controlled Temperament*. In LaHaye's book, she learned that you couldn't earn your salvation. Instead, all you had to do was believe that God loved the world so much that He gave his only Son so that everyone who believes in Him might not perish but have eternal life. Tim LaHaye's point was that when Jesus came into your life, He could change certain aspects of your personality.

"His message impacted me because all of a sudden, I had a hunger to read His Word and be around other Christians, whereas I had never wanted to do such things before," she said. "I had been raised a Christian, but my family didn't go to church much when I was growing up. My idea of being a Christian was doing the best you could in life and hope that would be good enough to make it into heaven. The book introduced me to Jesus in a way I had never heard before."

That's when she opened her eyes to Jesus and accepted Him as her savior.

She sought out my counterpart on the women's tour, Jenny Geddes. The woman's chaplain was a blessing to Cami, and they became best friends. "I was so thankful that Jenny was there to lead Bible studies and organize Christian housing for me," Cami said.

Cami and I met at the Grand Slam tournaments. I always thought she had a lot of potential, and she did become a Top 30 player. She remained in the Top 100 for six years, but after the age of twenty-three, Cami struggled to play in the top tournaments. She sought out a coach to turn things around, but he changed her swing and grip, which only messed her up even more. "It was a nightmare, and I was never the same. If I have a regret in tennis, it would be the time I changed my game."

Cami liked playing in Germany, and during her last two years as a touring professional, she played club tennis in Germany. Many Americans don't know that German tennis clubs hire professional players to play for them in various leagues. It's a big deal over there.

The first year she played in Leimen (Boris Becker's hometown), where everyone seemed to speak English, but when she returned for second season of Regionalliga tennis, she was contracted to play for a club in the former East German city of Leipzig, where no one spoke English. (They had all learned Russian in school.)

So . . . Cami had to learn German — in a hurry. She bought a German/English dictionary and gave herself a goal of learning ten words a night. In three weeks, she was speaking pretty good German.

When Cami retired from professional tennis after fourteen years on the road, she wanted to attend college and get the degree she missed by turning pro early. Education had always been important to her, and she had been a good student in high school. Cami was accepted at UCLA, where she took German 5 and 6 to improve her language skills and had a double major in psychology and communications. She also received a minor in German and graduated *summa cum laude*.

After finishing up at UCLA, she applied for and won a Fulbright scholarship to return to Germany as a graduate student. The Fulbright scholarship was good for one year, but she stayed in Germany for the next four years to complete a master's degree in psychology — in German.

"I think this is an important accomplishment, especially as an African-American," Cami said, "because so many black athletes never finish their schooling, and it is *such* an important thing to help build a future and be able to give back to the community."

While in Germany, she met her husband, Aaron Schermerhorn, online through eHarmony, and she moved back to the States to marry him six years ago. They live in Eugene, Oregon, where she is a qualified mental health professional (QMHP), working with kids. She still keeps a hand in tennis, teaching juniors ten hours a week.

She's careful, though, about making wholesale changes in swings and grips because she wants her students to play with some individuality.

Who knows . . . maybe there's another Cami Whammy out there.

After Robin and I became engaged, we posed for this fun photo. Robin became my partner in ministry as we traveled together to tournaments around the world.

11
BREAK POINT

In late 1986, Freeman Springer, woke up at 3 a.m., wide awake. Something was heavy on his heart—his daughter, Robin.

It wasn't that she was flunking out of college, in deep financial trouble, or running with the wrong crowd. Just the opposite. She was a godly young woman working as the Director of Public Relations for Coral Ridge Ministries, which produced a Sunday morning television show featuring the sermons of D. James Kennedy, an influential pastor and founder of Coral Ridge Presbyterian Church in Fort Lauderdale, Florida. *The Coral Ridge Hour* was syndicated on hundreds of stations worldwide and had a peak audience of three million viewers in 200 countries.

Freeman's daughter was a beautiful, head-turning redhead who stood five-feet, nine inches tall. She was also thirty years old and had never been married. In fact, she hadn't dated much because her standards were so high. She was pure and willing to wait—for the right guy to marry.

Next to his bed in the darkness, Freeman got on his knees

and prayed. "Lord, I lift up Robin to you," he whispered as his wife, Christie, slept. "She's followed You all her life and knows that You have plans to prosper her and not to harm her, plans to give her hope and a future. Lord, I humbly ask that You bring her a husband. I pray this in the name of Jesus, Amen."

Several months later, Robin was having dinner with a close friend named Vicky and her boyfriend, Jeff. They were chitchatting about various topics when Robin casually mentioned that she was discipling a young female tennis player who had recently moved from California.

Tennis?

Hearing that word prompted Jeff to blurt out, "You should meet Fritz Glaus."

Robin and I met on a blind date orchestrated by our friends Jeff and Vicky

Robin grimaced. Friends and acquaintances were always trying to set her up, and this guy with a funny-sounding German name didn't sound like the pick of the litter to her.

"Does he speak English?" she asked.

"Oh, Fritz is an American," Jeff said. "I know Fritz through Eddie Waxer. We did some ministry things together. He's a great guy. I think you should meet him."

"I'm not so sure . . ."

Jeff would not be deterred. "Listen, Fritz is a chaplain on the men's tennis tour, and they're playing down in Key Biscayne right now. The timing is perfect. Let us introduce him to you."

"How tall is he?" At five-feet, nine inches, Robin wasn't interested in dating someone she looked down upon.

"He's tall—over six feet. I'd say around six-two. Good-looking, too. You'll see."

Robin still wasn't convinced, but Jeff and Vicky promised that she wouldn't be wasting her time. They suggested taking Robin to the Miami Sea Aquarium the following day for a meet-and-greet—if they could reach me. If nothing worse, they said, Robin would see come colorful fish.

Robin relented, and Jeff tracked me down at the player's hotel. This was in early March in 1987, and I was thirty-two years old. Let's face it: when you're a tennis chaplain, you're signing up for long run of celibacy. I could count the number of dates in the last ten years, going back to my Peter Burwash years, on a single hand. Not that I wasn't greatly interested in marrying—I was—but I was following a more important call at the moment.

Okay, call it a "blind date" of sorts, but why not take a shot? We met at noon at the Miami Sea Aquarium, and my attraction bells sounded a three-engine alarm. It was like time stood still—and there was no one else strolling the grounds of the aquarium. I have no idea what happened to Jeff and Vicky, but Robin and I sat down and talked for three hours without interruption—sharing our backgrounds, sharing our lives, and sharing our hopes for the future. She wanted to know all about life on the men's tour, and I wanted to know what it was like working with Dr. Kennedy because I'd seen him preach on TV.

Toward four o'clock, I knew I should get back to the Lipton tournament, but I couldn't let her go.

"What are you doing tonight?" I hoped to ask her to a player's party that evening.

"I'm invited to a barbecue with some friends," she said.

My heart sank.

"Oh, that's too bad. There's a player's party that you could come to, meet some of the guys . . ."

Robin gathered her thoughts. "Hey, could you come up to my party later?"

Could I? "Of course, I can," I said. I was already crazy about this girl.

I arrived late to her friend's barbecue in the Fort Lauderdale area. When I stepped into the backyard, I saw her speaking to a guy, and my heart sank again. I hoped that wasn't her boyfriend.

When she saw me, her eyes lit up—and I knew she was free of entanglements. We became an item that night.

The next day, she called her dad and told him all about me. "If I don't marry this guy, I'll be really surprised," she said.

We kept in touch as best as we could. I'd call her frequently from tournaments played in the U.S., and when the circuit moved to Europe for the clay court and grass court seasons, I sent her postcards and made periodic — and expensive — overseas phone calls. We made plans for her to join me in London just before the start of the Wimbledon fortnight.

I thought it would be fun to show her some castles in the south of England, so we took a little driving trip with plans to stay at a "guest house" — private homes where people put a sign out offering rooms to the public. Kind of like the *Zimmer Frei* signs you see when driving around Germany.

We stopped at a charming cottage near the thousand-year-old Arundel Castle, complete with a dry moat and filled with priceless works of art, and inquired about the availability of two bedrooms.

The man of the house looked at me, then looked at Robin. "Why do you each want your own room?" he asked.

"Because we're not married," I replied.

The man looked perplexed. "This is some sort of joke, right?"

"No. We want separate bedrooms."

He kept trying to get us to take one bedroom. I gently but firmly repeated that we wanted two bedrooms. He sighed and finally relented.

We had a great time romping through the countryside, visiting Tudor castles and poking around antique stores. Then Robin flew back to the States shortly before the tournament started. She could see that I had a lot going on.

The players receive all sorts of goodies from the tournament, including theater tickets by the bushel. I had several players — after they lost — give me a bunch of tickets to London's best shows because they couldn't use them. I then passed them along to parents of players who were still in the draw or to families who had volunteered to house Christian players.

One father and mother of a son who played in the tournament were grateful to receive tickets to a hot show that had opened a year earlier—Andrew Lloyd Webber's *Phantom of the Opera*. The follow day, the couple sought me out to thank me for the extraordinary show.

"Hey, Fritz," said the father. "We have a cabin in Winter Park, Colorado. You're welcome to use it anytime you want. Do you need a vacation place to stay?"

I pondered that for a moment. "Actually, I might be looking for a honeymoon spot," I said.

"Then you've got a place," said the dad.

By the time I got to New York for the U.S. Open, my closest friends knew I was itching to ask Robin to marry me. A New York City diamond jeweler that I had met approached me about getting a pair of box seats for "Super Saturday," a tennis smorgasbord when the two men's semifinals were sandwiched around the women's finals. I didn't have any tickets, but I said I'd check around. That's when Gene Mayer said he'd take care of him.

Lo and behold, the diamond jeweler and Gene worked out a little side deal: Gene would get him two great seats for Super Saturday and also give him three tennis rackets and the diamond dealer would give me a soul deal on a diamond engagement ring and wedding band.

I think I paid one-third the normal price for a beautiful engagement ring and jeweled wedding band for Robin. After the U.S. Open was over, I flew down to Fort Lauderdale. That evening, I asked if she wanted to go for a walk on the beach. I got down on one knee and proposed to her, and she said yes. I presented her with the ring, and even though she couldn't see the brilliant diamonds in the dark, she was crying tears of happiness.

Nothing like a friendly tennis match or two before the big wedding. Participating were (from the left) Mike Leach, Rob Reichel, Dr. D. James Kennedy of Coral Ridge Presbyterian Church in Fort Lauderdale, Florida, myself, and my college doubles partner, Chris Ramsberg.

A star-studded cast joined Robin and me for our marriage: (from left front) Fritz Glaus Sr., Bud Cox, Stan Smith, Greg Williams, Chris Ramsberg, Mike Leach, Ben Testerman, Hal Schaus, Rob Reichel, and in the forefront, my childhood friend, Jeff Niedenthal and his son, Jared.

I felt like I was the most blessed man in the world
when I married Robin.

We honeymooned in the Colorado Rockies resort village of Winter Park at the start of the ski season.

Robin immediately fit in with the girls on the tour: (from the left) Gretchen Magers, an English player whose name escapes us, Cami Benjamin, Carol Fullerton, and Robin.

We were married by Dr. Kennedy in Fort Lauderdale on Saturday, November 28, 1987, two days after Thanksgiving. After an amazing wedding night together, we flew the next day to Denver, Colorado, where we drove to our honeymoon nest in the Colorado Rockies.

Upon our arrival in Winter Park, we stepped inside a beautiful mountain home with a fully stocked refrigerator filled with food and drinks. We had a great week and loved skiing by day and getting cozy on the cold, snowy nights.

Traveling the Tour with Robin

Robin proved to be a great "help meet," as Genesis 2:18 describes how God made a companion for Adam. She was a real plus with the player's wives, who appreciated that they had someone to talk to, and with the women players when both tours were playing at the same site.

We were inseparable throughout 1988, 1989, and most of the 1990 season. She didn't join me for a three-week trip to Germany, where I spoke to the Sportler-ruft-Sportler staff and athletes during a three-day conference. I'm sure my half-German, half-English talks were hilarious to their ears, but the folks in sports ministry wanted to hear about the tennis tour and what I did.

I flew home to Cleveland, about fifty miles from our home base in Akron, and Robin greeted me with a warm kiss and bouquet of pink and blue balloons at the airport gate. After eleven hours in the airplane, I was bushed. It was four a.m. for me.

"What are the balloons for?" I asked. She had never greeted me like that before.

Robin figured out that I was doing the typical male clueless act.

"Don't you know?

"Know what?"

"We're having a baby!" she exclaimed.

Our joy, however, would soon turn into one of the most difficult struggles of our lives. I'll let Robin explain.

Even in Darkness, Light Dawns on the Upright

When we left for Europe in April, I (Robin) was three months pregnant and had a clean bill of health from the doctor. Little did we know what lay ahead.

The day our announcement was to go out to ask for prayers and to share the joy with our friends and supporters, I started spotting. Having just arrived in France only two days before, we knew no one and spoke no French. We were staying in the home of a family who was on holiday in America for a month, so we were all alone in a small town, way out in the country.

I was scared. Contractions began as the bleeding became heavier. We didn't know where a hospital was, how to call an emergency vehicle, or how to tell anyone where we were staying.

By 4 a.m., the pain was unbearable. Who could we call? Fritz found the number of an American businessman that we had met at a church the day before.

"Bob, this is Fritz. I'm sorry to wake you up, but I think my wife is having a miscarriage. Do you know where there's a hospital?"

"I have the name of a hospital in Cannes, but I can't tell you how to get there," Bob said. "Let me give you the number of a pastor I know. He can give you directions."

Oh, great. We have to wake someone else up.

Within minutes I was wrapped in a blanket and helped to

the car, praying all the way. I cried.

The directions the pastor gave us were . . . "Turn right as you come into town . . . " but where? There were no hospital signs, no Jiffy Stores or 24-hour gas stations. The town closes down at 11 p.m. At that moment, we passed some street sweepers. Fritz yelled out the window, "Hospital!"

"No English," someone yelled back.

"Hospital, hospital," Fritz yelled again. They pointed to the street on our right. Right there, right at that corner, right at that moment! *Lord, did you put them there just for us? Thank you!*

When we arrived at the hospital, none of the night staff spoke English. Fritz tried to communicate, but it was impossible.

Suddenly a voice behind us said, in English, "Can I help you?" It was Keith, the pastor.

"I thought you might need someone to translate," he said.

"Thank you, God!"

After the initial exam, I was wheeled to the maternity ward to await further examination and testing. The only vacant bed was in a room shared by a young woman who had been a nanny in America. She interpreted for me as the doctors and nurses came and went. God's hand was evident.

The ultrasound showed that the baby had never grown past two weeks and they would have to do a D&C. I walked back to the room, alone. "Lord, I am so disappointed," I cried.

Where are the comfort Psalms? I wondered. Psalm 23 was the only one I could think of, and that didn't touch where I was hurting that day. *Lord, what should I read?* Immediately Psalm 112 came to mind. I didn't remember reading that before . . .

Praise the Lord! Blessed is the man who fears the Lord, who finds great delight in his commands. His children will be mighty in the land; each generation of the upright will be blessed . . . Even in darkness, light dawns for the upright, for the gracious and compassionate and righteous man. Good will come to him . . . Surely he will never be shaken . . . He will have no fear of bad news: his heart is steadfast, trusting in the Lord. His heart is secure, he will have no fear; in the end he will look on his foes in triumph.

When Fritz came in, we cried and prayed and held each other. God's hand was so evident. His fingerprints were everywhere. We knew He was near.

The first thing I saw when I woke from surgery was an empty bassinet beside my bed. Tears began to flow as I thought of the joy most women who stayed in this room experienced. But it was not my turn. God had other plans for me . . . deeper lessons of his grace, faithfulness, and provision. It was a session in the school of sorrow.

More than any time in our lives, Fritz and I experienced the reality of being "carried" by God. The pain was real, but there was a calm and comfort, which touched that spot deep inside where no human could. We experienced the power of prayer as many of our friends lifted us up to the Lord and the uniqueness of the body of Christ as new friends in France ministered to us. Indeed, ". . . even in darkness, light dawns on the upright."

A Child Is Born

Robin explained it perfectly. Even in darkness, light dawns. A year after we left for Europe, Garrett Ryan Glaus was born on April 17, 1991.

Robin stayed home that summer while I went to Roland Garros and Wimbledon, but being apart was hard. Garrett traveled with us the following year, and his first international trip was to Wimbledon, where we returned for the annual backyard party hosted by Mark and Iona Birchall. Midway through the party, Iona tugged at my elbow and pulled me aside.

She looked me in the eyes and held my gaze. "Your fire is gone," she said. "This is probably your last year."

She was right. You can't travel around the world with a little baby. It was too difficult for mother and child to get on any sort of routine—and babies love routine. The reality of traveling full time with a young child was setting in, and we both knew change was inevitable.

I met with my board of directors after the U.S. Open. A half-dozen godly men like pastors Dave Burnham and Randy Pope and former players like Stan Smith and Gene Mayer had been on my board over the years, and they had a lot of wisdom.

The handwriting on the wall was there in large, bold script. Every year it was getting harder and harder to raise the money to keep my family and myself out on the tour. Tennis ministry was expensive. I had to stay in the player's hotels so that I would be instantly and easily available to meet with anyone who wanted to see me. By 1992, the tour had matured to the point where three-star and four-star accommodations didn't cut it any longer. The player's hotels were always top-drawer, five-star places. When you added in the meals, plane tickets, car rentals, and train rides—the budget to keep us on the road was substantial.

More importantly, though, the composition of the tour had changed in the last dozen years. When I started in 1980, there were forty-eight Americans in the Wimbledon draw of 128 and six of the eight quarterfinalists were Americans. At the 1980 U.S. Open, there were *seventy* players in the 128-person draw and half the quarterfinalists were Americans.

During my final year on the tour in 1992, there had been a noticeable attrition rate of Americans playing on the tour. At the 1992 Wimbledon event, there were twenty-five Americans in the draw—a drop of nearly 50 percent. For the 1992 U.S. Open, there were thirty-four Americans in the draw—again about a 50 percent drop from 12 years previously.

No longer was the tour made up of primarily Americans and Australians with a smattering of French, German, Spanish, and Italian players. Tennis had gone global, and the number of players from different countries was staggering. That trend has continued to today. I looked at the draws of the recent Wimbledon and U.S. Open championships, and the number of Americans in the tournament were under fifteen, even ten players. At the U.S. Open, nearly half the Americans playing in the tournament received wild cards, meaning their ranking wasn't high enough to get straight in.

It's hard to make friends, share the Gospel, or sustain long-lasting relationships with someone who doesn't share your mother tongue. Sure, English is the *de facto* official language on the tour, but the players don't learn words like *grace, salvation,* and *the gospel* growing up. Their vocabulary revolves around words like *challenge, overrule,* and *What you mean, the ball was out?* Nearly all of today's players have grown up in secular cultures and have only a vague idea about Jesus Christ or what the Good News of the Gospel means, which requires a different approach to reach out to them.

Back in 1992, it was becoming clearer with each passing week that my time on the tour was drawing to an end. With great reluctance, my board directed me to stop doing the tennis ministry at the end of the year.

It was not a good day when the board closed our doors. We were hurt, heartbroken, and upset and had no idea what we would do next. Robin and I viewed this as the death of a vision, and though we knew we couldn't keep things going the way they were, we weren't ready to give up the tennis ministry just yet.

But we had to. Hal Schaus, my mentor at The Chapel, offered to help me make the transition to "civilian life." Think about the circumstances: I was thirty-eight years old and hadn't led a normal life when I was on the tour. The working world doesn't go to bed at one or two in the morning and sleep until 10 or 11 o'clock. But those are the hours that the players kept because they didn't have to play until the afternoon or evening. Hal was a psychotherapist, and he spent several days talking things through to me about what adjustments I would need to make to become accustomed to "normal" life.

After I left the tour, I taught tennis in Orlando for two years, and then coached two years in Redwood City, California, not far from San Francisco. By then I was in my early forties and a second child, Parker, had arrived. Back in the old Peter Burwash days, I could teach eight, nine hours a day, no problem. Now my body was rebelling. My back was continually sore, tennis elbow was setting in, and I was just drained at the end of the day. Physically, I didn't see how I could continue teaching tennis into my fifties and sixties.

I changed careers and got into financial advising and have worked with different companies in Charlotte for the last eleven years. Meanwhile, I was glad to be an involved father with Garrett and Parker, helping to raise them to love the Lord and live for Him. Robin and I want the boys to follow their passion and develop their unique gifts. These days,

Garrett is into music, and Parker is a baseball player.

All four of us are actively involved in a church that has exploded to more than 10,000 members in just six years. The church, called Elevation, is where we hear Pastor Steve Furtick share a message of audacious faith and how to approach every experience from a visionary perspective, seeing God in all of life. The boys are always inviting their friends to join us, which is pretty cool.

Seeds Were Planted

The memories of the years I spent on the men's tennis tour are fading like an old colored photograph, but as I look back, it was amazing to think about how I met Stan Smith and then Eddie Waxer . . . and how God directed everything to give me—a simple kid from Brewster, Ohio, a chance to minister to some of the most high-profile athletes in the world. Think about it: a tennis chaplaincy is not a job you find in the classified ads. God found me, and I'm eternally grateful for the opportunity to speak into player's lives and plant seeds of hope and faith in Christ.

And that's all I did—plant seeds. Once those seeds are sown, it's up to God to make sure the growth happens.

I understand the Parable of the Sower much better now. In this story told by Christ to his apostles, a farmer went out into the field to sow his seed. And as he sowed seed, some fell on rocky ground, some fell among thorns, and some fell on good soil—all with various results.

In a similar fashion, I was a sower of seeds on the men's professional tour. Sure, some of the seeds I threw fell by the wayside—among players who showed no interest in learning how Jesus died for their sins so that they could have eternal life. Other seeds failed to penetrate the stony hearts of many players, which prevented the Word from making an impression. But I would say that most of my seeds fell amid the thorns, meaning that these seeds took root for a while, even changed players' lives for a season, but the riches and pleasures of life on the tour choked their growth. I saw that happen time and time again.

That grieves me, but I prefer to remember the seeds that fell on good soil, which grew and brought forth fruit a hundred times over. Although this didn't happen many times, seeing players' lives change made it worth all the effort.

You see, it was my job—my ministry—to share God's love and grace with whoever would listen—"whoever has ears to hear, let him hear"—and pray that the seeds of God's message of salvation would pierce their hearts.

Many seeds were sown during twelve seasons on the men's professional tennis tour. I guess I won't know what happened to most of those seeds until that Day when I meet Jesus Christ in glory.

Mike Yorkey, my co-author for *Love Game*, married his wife,
Nicole, at a castle outside of Zurich, Switzerland in 1979.
As they departed a small chapel on the grounds, they were
greeted by members of the Wettingen Tennis Club,
who held rackets aloft to form an arc.

12
CONSOLATION BRACKET
Ten Matches to Borg by Mike Yorkey

Note from Fritz: *My co-writer, Mike Yorkey, never played on the ATP Tour, but through an amazing set of circumstances, he did play the French Open qualification tournament while honeymooning in Paris back in 1979. I thought I'd finish* Love Game *by having Mike tell his engaging story of how he — a club player from California — found himself in the Roland Garros qualies. And what's equally fascinating to me is that Mike's wife, Nicole, is also from Switzerland.*

Every May marks the anniversary of two special events in my life: the day I married my wife, Nicole, and the day I played the French Open qualifications during our honeymoon in Paris in 1979. As I'm fond of telling our children, I was only ten defaults away from playing Bjorn Borg for my first Grand Slam title.

For sure, as the Angelic Assassin liked to say, some amazing things would have had to have happened before I strolled onto Court Central at 15:00 hours on Roland Garros' second Sunday. I would have needed ten walkovers to get there: opponents tripping over the nailed sidelines and breaking their ankles, severe ptomaine poisoning, wake-up calls that never happened, and courtesy cars traveling in circles in the Bois de Boulogne.

That's because I didn't deserve to tie the white shoelaces on Bjorn's Tretorn sneakers. I was what you'd call a "club player"—a twenty-five-year-old tennis enthusiast good enough to play college tennis at the University of Oregon, but someone who was also first-round fodder in "open" tournaments back in my home state of California. A touring pro appraising my game would charitably say that I couldn't hit the ball.

So how did I find myself on the salmon-colored *terre batue* of Paris, in the French Open qualification draw no less, with a pathway to Court Central?

My story begins at Mammoth Mountain, a ski resort in California's Eastern Sierra mountains, where I met Nicole Schmied of Switzerland, who was teaching skiing for a season to improve her English—her fifth language. We quickly fell in love, and not only was Nicole a great skier, but she came from a tennis family in Switzerland and could really play.

We were married at a 13th century castle—Schloss Böttstein—outside of Zurich. As we bounded down the aisle of the medieval chapel, we stepped outside, only to be warmly greeted by members of the Wettingen Tennis Club, who were holding tennis rackets aloft, forming an arc for us to pass under.

At the reception, I chatted with John Savage, a buddy who flew to Switzerland for the nuptials—and ran me around the tennis court that morning. John owned a tennis shop in La Jolla, a San Diego suburb, where he strung rackets for Pat DuPre, then a Top 20 player.

When John told Pat about his upcoming trip to Europe, Pat offered to make a phone call to try to get John into the qualification tournament for the Championnats International de France—known as Roland Garros today—slated to begin one week after my wedding.

I informed John that since we would be honeymooning in Paris at the same time, we'd love to see him play. John was a better player than me; he usually survived until the third round of open tournaments in San Diego. "Maybe Pat can get you into the qualies, too," John said.

Believe it or not, his idea didn't seem that farfetched to me. John and I had heard tales of tournament directors filling their qualification draw sheets with the flotsam of the tennis circuit. Back in 1979, tennis had been "open" for only eleven years, and the infrastructure supporting the game was barely beyond the foundation stage. The computer rankings to determine fair entry conditions into tournaments had only been around since 1973, but often times—especially at the more obscure tournaments in far-flung locales—any holes in the draw sheet were filled purely on a first-come, first-served basis.

Later that evening, I told Nicole about the plan that John and I had hatched. Of course, trying to play the French Open qualifications meant a slight change in our honeymoon plans. Since Paris was our first stop, couldn't John tag along?

The idea of honeymooning in Paris in a *ménage à trois* did not sit well with Nicole. Nothing like having your first marriage crisis on your wedding night.

"But John doesn't speak any French, and you do," I told her. "Think of poor John."

"Think of me," she replied.

Imagine my wife's feelings when the three of us waved goodbye to her parents at the Baden train station, bound for the City of Light.

We arrived in Paris several days before the qualifying tournament, giving Nicole and myself—plus John—time to take in the sights of one of the most beautiful cities in the world. We eyed hundreds of fat angels at the Louvre. Ate *baguettes de jambon* on the banks of the River Seine. Checked out the kitschy paintings at Montmarte. Rode the dizzying Métro everywhere.

Then, one morning, John and I struck out for the Bois de Boulogne and Stade Roland Garros, site of the French Open. The tournament didn't start for another five days, but when we arrived, orange-garbed workmen were raising blue-and-white striped sponsors' tents and sweeping the grounds with witch-like brooms. Maintenance teams pushed antiquated rollers and sprayed water over the famous clay courts.

We were directed to offices underneath the grandstands of Court Central. Armed with my limited high school French, we had a difficult time conveying what we wanted. Finally, we were led to a small office, where a young tennis official was seated behind a desk.

"What can I do for you?" he asked in accented English.

"We are from California," I stammered, "and we're here to play in the French Open qualification tournament. Pat DuPre said he would call for us."

"Who?"

"Pat DuPre. He's an American player, beat Jimmy Connors last—"

"Do you have a world ranking?"

John and I gave each other a blank look. "No," I replied.

"A United States ranking."

We both shook our heads.

Silence filled the room. "Ah, is there a waiting list we could put our names on?" I stammered.

The French tennis official replied with a Gallic shrug. He looked around his desk, found an old envelope, and handed it to us. We printed our names on the back, and as we left, I thought I heard a wad of paper land in the *poubelle*.

The meeting was not a total loss. On a bulletin board was information that the qualifying tournament, to be held the next day, was *not* at Roland Garros but at a different tennis club about a kilometer away. Maybe some of the qualifiers will get lost trying to find the place, I told John. We agreed that it was still worth a try.

The next morning it was lucky that Nicole accompanied us because we got lost trying to find the club and arrived twenty minutes after the 9 a.m. deadline. Scores of players in Adidas warm-ups formed a Maginot line around the tournament desk. The din of a dozen languages filled the room. I tried to propel myself toward the front, but I was rebuffed every time.

Thirty minutes later, the crowd slackened. I darted to the front and caught the gaze of a French tennis official, who I later learned was Jacques Dorfman. In English, I explained that we were on the waiting list for the qualifiers. Were we in the draw?

Dorfman asked me to spell my name. I waved for John. A moment later, Dorfman swept up a half-dozen draw sheets and walked into a side room, followed by a retinue of officials.

We killed time with Brad Rowe, an up-and-coming player from San Diego. Since the main draw of the French Open was 128 players, Brad explained, the tournament's qualification draw had to be 128, too. "That's a big draw for a qualification tournament," said Brad. "Win four matches, get to the quarters, and you're in the main draw." *Yeah, right.*

The draw sheets were finally posted, and, like schoolboys poring over test results, we searched for our names. When I found my name etched on the draw sheet, I felt as if I was going to lose my breakfast croissant.

I was the third match of the day on Court 17, the court farthest away from the locker room. That was fine with me. John was scheduled for Court 16.

I found a backboard and began beating the wall feverishly, as if to make up for lost time. I had played only a few times in the past month because of all the wedding preparations.

When John was called to his match, I caught a glimpse of his opponent—an Ecuadorian in his late thirties who carried a single racquet strung with cheap blue twist nylon. As they began warming up, the South American couldn't break an egg with his softball strokes. Was there really someone worse than John or me in the draw?

"*Monsieur Yor-kay, Monsieur Yor-kay,*" blared the crackling loudspeaker. At the tournament desk, I was told to report to Court 17. My gait stiffened as I walked onto the court, behind a French tennis umpire, several linesmen, and a crew of green-shirted ball boys.

It turned out my opponent, Sam West, was from California, too. During a nervous warm-up, I was thankful I wasn't on some show court playing Antonio Zugarelli or Eric Van Dillen, two of the "name players" I saw in the qualifying draw. I actually believed I could lose a "golden set" to one of those guys—24 straight points.

Imagine my surprise when I served and Sam sprayed the

first few returns out. Then I returned the favor on his serve. After I held serve a couple of more times, the umpire intoned, *"Jeu, Monsieur Yor-kay. Il mene, trois jeux à deux, premier manche."*

I was living a hacker's dream. During the changeover leading 2-3, I wiped my forehead with a French Open towel — and soaked up the atmosphere as well. The ball boys rolled balls from one end of the court to the other. The linesmen sat quietly in their seats, staring straight ahead. A few people, including my wife, watched from the sidelines. In the background, the ironclad Eiffel Tower loomed in the gray sky.

My game came back to the red earth when Sam started playing better. I began making a lot of errors, and my opponent swept the first set, 6-3. Undaunted, I broke serve in the first game of the second set with a backhand winner down the line. I almost did a Connors-like strut, but I caught myself.

I envisioned a storied comeback, of winning the match, of being one step closer to Bjorn Borg.

Except I didn't win another game.

Meanwhile, on the next court, John won the first set in a tiebreaker. But this old coot was playing John like a metronome: drop shot, lob; drop shot, lob. John couldn't run anymore — he was out of *essence*. The second and third sets went quietly.

As we showered in the players' locker room, John and I started laughing. We had pulled it off, at the French Open, no less. Little did we know that our Cinderella story would be as improbable today as someone playing a Grand Slam qualification tournament with a wood racket, gut strings, and white tennis balls.

ABOUT MIKE YORKEY

Mike Yorkey is the author, co-author, editor or collaborator of more than 75 books, including these collaborative efforts:

• *Believe: The Eric LeGrand Story*, the story of Rutgers football player Eric LeGrand, who was paralyzed from the neck down on a kickoff play in 2010.
• *My Big Greek Fat Diet* by Nick Yphantides, M.D., who lost 270 pounds
• *Play Ball* by former San Francisco Giant pitcher Dave Dravecky
• *Holding Serve* by tennis star Michael Chang
• *Every Man's Battle* by Steve Arterburn and Fred Stoeker (there are nine books in this series that has sold 2 million copies)
• *The Act of Marriage After 40* by Tim and Beverly LaHaye (Tim co-authored the most successful fiction series of all time, the *Left Behind* series)
• *Perfect Weight America* by Jordan Rubin (he has written 22 books for health expert Jordan Rubin)
• *Fit Over 40 Dummies* by Betsy McCormack (wife of Mark McCormack, the founder of IMG, the largest sports agency in the world)
• *Unglued & Tattooed: How to Save Your Teen from Raves, Ritalin, Goth, Body Carving, GHB, Sex, and 12 Other Emerging Threats* by Sara Trollinger, founder of the House of Hope in Orlando, Florida
• *Don't Date Naked* by Michael and Amy Smalley
• *Up, Up and Away: The Story of Marilyn McCoo and Billy Davis Jr.* (they were part of the Sixties music group, The Fifth Dimension)
• *The Essentials of Highly Healthy Teens* by Walt Larimore, M.D.

Mike Yorkey grew up in La Jolla, California, and graduated from the University of Oregon with a B.S. degree from the School of Journalism in 1975. After a stint as a newspaper editor, he was editor of *Focus on the Family* magazine from 1986-1997 and also held other titles at Focus on the Family, including editorial director and editor-in-chief.

As editor of *Focus on the Family* magazine, he probably wrote and edited 1,000 articles. More than 200 million copies of *Focus on the Family* magazine were published during his tenure. In addition, he has written for *The Los Angeles Times Travel Section, Skiing, Tennis, World Tennis, City Sports,* and *Racquet.*

Mike has been married 33 years to Nicole, a native of Switzerland. They are the parents of two adult children, Andrea and Patrick. The Yorkeys make their home in Encinitas, California.

His website is www.mikeyorkey.com.

Made in the USA
Charleston, SC
22 August 2012